Invitational Learning
for
Counseling
and
Development

William W. F
John J. Sch

and

Gary C. Benedict
Joel Blackburn
Debbie Chance
Judy Lehr

Donald E. McBrien
Cheryl French Stehle
John H. Wilson

ERIC Counseling and Personnel Services Clearinghouse
2108 School of Education
The University of Michigan
Ann Arbor, Michigan 48109-1259

ERIC Counseling and Personnel Services Clearinghouse
2108 School of Education
The University of Michigan
Ann Arbor, MI 48109-1259

ISBN 1-56109-002-6

This publication was prepared with partial funding from the Office of Educational Research and Improvement, U.S. Department of Education under contract no. RI88062011. The opinions expressed in this report do not necessarily reflect the positions or policies of OERI, the Department of Education, or ERIC/CAPS.

Contents

Introduction

It is a pleasure to welcome Dr. Purkey's and Dr. Schmidt's *Invitational Learning for Counseling and Development* to the crème de la crème series—the **best** of the best. It was not a difficult choice as Dr. Purkey's Invitational Learning has been utilized in a variety of school settings and the result is almost always the same—a significant change in the school environment and how students and school faculty behave.

This volume is distinguished from previous writings on Invitational Learning in two significant ways. First, Purkey and Schmidt have expanded and enhanced their perspective and concepts to include the work of the counselor. In any school setting, the counselor is in a pivotal position to positively influence the adoption and use of Invitational Learning by all school personnel. Grounded as they are in self-concept theory, counselors can readily understand the rationale behind Invitational Learning and imaginatively implement the concepts into counseling and the curriculum. Counselors are also in an excellent position to serve as consultants to school faculty on how Invitational Learning can transform classrooms and the school into more rewarding and achievement nurturing places to be.

Secondly, this volume differs from previous writing on Invitational Learning in that school-based contributors speak in straightforward tones about how they used Invitational Learning in their varied settings and with what results. Their excitement and pleasure about what they are doing is infectious and provides the reader with a motivational "jump start" to get going on making changes in their school as well as offering practical, field-tested approaches that offer a high probability of success.

I am often a bit wary of good writers. They can make difficult tasks seem so easy. But it never quite works out that way for me: Making changes almost always seems more difficult than the text implies. Purkey and Schmidt are a rare exception. They excite you. They motivate you. And, most importantly, they show you how to proceed. I strongly expect that anyone who reads and uses this volume will agree that it has changed for the better and forever how they approach counseling and schooling.

And that is the reason we welcome the addition of this volume to the crème de la crème series.

Garry R. Walz
Director, ERIC/CAPS

About the Authors

William W. Purkey is Professor of Counselor Education at the University of North Carolina at Greensboro and Co–Director of the International Alliance for Invitational Education. Dr. Purkey is an active writer, lecturer, and researcher and has written more than 80 articles and five books including *Self-Concept and School Achievement* now in its 18th printing. He is also the recipient of many awards including the Good Teaching Award from the Standard Oil Foundation and the 1989 Professional Development Award presented by the American Association for Counseling and Development. He has been a public school teacher and an instructor in the United States Air Force as well as a university professor.

John J. Schmidt is Associate Professor of Counselor Education and Acting Chair of the Department of Counselor and Adult Education at East Carolina University in Greenville, North Carolina. He has written numerous articles for counseling and education journals and is co–author of the book *The Inviting Relationship: An Expanded Perspective for Professional Counseling*. Dr. Schmidt was named North Carolina Elementary School Counselor of the Year in 1978 and received the Professional Writing and Research Award from the North Carolina Association for Counseling and Development in 1988. He has served on the Editorial Board of the journal *Elementary School Guidance and Counseling* and recently edited a special issue on middle school counseling for the journal *American Middle School Education*.

Contributors

Gary C. Benedict is Superintendent of the Affton School District in St. Louis, Missouri. He is the author of over 100 articles in professional journals. During his 29 years in the field of education he has been a teacher, principal, assistant superintendent, superintendent, and adjunct college lecturer.

Joel Blackburn is Principal of Sugar Loaf School in Taylorsville, North Carolina. In 1987 Sugar Loaf School was the recipient of the "Inviting School Award" from the Alliance for Invitational Education.

Debbie Chance is an Assistant Principal at East Davidson High School in Thomasville, North Carolina. She is also a doctoral student in educational administration at the University of North Carolina at Greensboro.

Judy Lehr is an Assistant Professor of Education at Furman University in Greenville, South Carolina and directs the university's Center of Excellence—a program to prepare educators to effectively work with at-risk students. She has led seminars and presented workshops at the state, national and international levels.

Donald E. McBrien is the Director of Pupil Services for Baltimore County Public Schools in Maryland and chairs the Ethical Review Board of the National Board of Certified Counselors. He is a charter member of the Alliance for Invitational Education and a past editor of the Alliance newsletter.

Cheryl French Stehle is the Director of Graduate Studies and Continuing Education for the University of South Carolina at Beaufort. She is a long-time member of the Alliance for Invitational Education and is also a contributing editor for *Islander Magazine* of Hilton Head Island, South Carolina.

John H. Wilson is Professor of Instructional Services at Wichita State University in Wichita, Kansas. He is author of the book *The Invitational Elementary Classroom*, co-author of two other books, and a frequent presenter at workshops and conferences.

Part I

The Theory:
Invitational Learning

I now believe there is no biological, geographical, social, economic, or psychological determiner of man's condition that he cannot transcend if he is suitably invited or challenged to do so.

Disclosing Man to Himself
—Sidney Jourard

Chapter 1

What Is Invitational Learning?

An idea whose time has come: the gradually formed and tested hypothesis that the individual has within himself vast resources for self-understanding, for altering his self-concept, his attitudes, and his self-directed behavior and that these resources can be tapped if only a definable climate of facilitative psychological attitudes can be provided.

In Retrospect-Forty-Six Years
—Carl Rogers

This monograph is about "a definable climate of facilitative psychological attitudes" that we have named "Invitational Learning." Invitational Learning takes a theoretical stance regarding the marvelous possibilities within each person and applies this stance in countless helping relationships designed to enrich existence and facilitate development. Simply stated, Invitational Learning offers a blueprint of what counselors, teachers, principals, supervisors, superintendents and others can do to enrich the physical and psychological environments of institutions and encourage the development of the people who live and work there.

Invitational Learning claims as its province the global nature of institutions, including people, places, policies, programs, and processes. These five "P's" in combination with other elements of Invitational Learning offer a paradigm for personal and professional functioning. The goal of Invitational Learning is to change the entire structure of organizations by building a foundation of respect, trust, optimism, and intentionality.

The concept of Invitational Learning was first introduced by Purkey (1978) and developed and refined by

Invitational Learning takes a theoretical stance regarding the marvelous possibilities within each person....

3

Purkey and Novak (1984), Purkey and Schmidt (1987), Wilson (1986), Strahan and Strahan (1988) and others. The invitational model has been applied in a variety of professional fields, including nursing (Ripley, 1986; Spikes, 1987), dental hygiene (Amos, 1985), counseling (Schmidt, 1982, 1988), administration (Purkey & Warters, 1986), and physical education (Chandler, 1988). The model has relevance to a number of concerns in counseling. For example, Invitational Learning can be applied to classroom management (Purkey & Strahan, 1986), school dropouts (Purkey & Stanley, 1989) and parenting (Purkey & Schmidt, 1982).

...Invitational Learning has been incorporated in hundreds of educational settings....

In addition to the educational programs featured in the second part of this monograph, Invitational Learning has been incorporated in hundreds of educational settings throughout the United States, Canada, and overseas. A list of these settings is presented in Appendix B. These have been recognized by the International Alliance for Invitational Education as exemplary in applying Invitational Learning.

The Alliance is a non-profit organization of professional educators and allied human service personnel who seek to apply the principles of Invitational Learning to promote positive change in organizational cultures, provide leadership in teaching, research, and service and to enrich the lives of human beings personally and professionally. Centers for the Alliance are located at the University of North Carolina at Greensboro and Brock University, Ontario, Canada. The Alliance was founded at LeHigh University in 1982 to further Invitational Education, of which Invitational Learning is an important part.

Invitational Learning is based on four value-laden assumptions regarding the nature of people and their potential and the nature of professional helping. These four overarching assumptions help to distinguish Invitational Learning from other approaches to helping. Should these assumptions be violated for any reason, the spirit of Invitational Learning is violated. The four assumptions are:

1. **Respect:** People are able, valuable, and responsible and should be treated accordingly.
2. **Trust:** Education should be a collaborative, cooperative activity where process is as important as product.

3. **Optimism:** People possess untapped potential in all areas of human endeavor.
4. **Intentionality:** Human potential can best be realized by places, policies, programs, and processes that are specifically designed to invite development, and by people who are intentionally inviting with themselves and others, personally and professionally.

These four assumptions will now be considered in detail.

Respect

Nothing in Invitational Learning is as important as the people in the process. The indispensable element in any successful organization is shared responsibility based on free and open discussion, cooperation, and mutual respect.

Outstanding businesses have long recognized the importance of respect in productive relationships. Respect for employees is one of the basic characteristics of excellent companies (Peters & Waterman, 1982). Conversely, one of the biggest complaints employees report is lack of recognition. The long-term success of any organization depends on the satisfaction of the people who live and work there. Such satisfaction is exemplified by behaviors that illustrate a positive attitude of "being with" as opposed to "doing to" perspectives. Central to this attitude is respect for the uniqueness and value of each human being. This respect is manifested in the caring and appropriate behaviors we exhibit as well as the places, policies, programs and processes we create and maintain.

The long-term success of any organization depends on the satisfaction of the people who live and work there.

Few relationships in life can be productive and helpful without respect for the integrity of the people involved. In professional counseling, for example, respect is sometimes a fragile quality because clients are frequently at an ebb point in their lives. They are desperately looking towards others to be "rescued" or "saved." But such actions are in opposition to Invitational Learning. To deny the person's authority over his or her own life, to take away the person's ultimate responsibility for his or her own existence, is disrespectful. No matter how much we would like people to do what we wish them to do, no matter how beneficial the desired actions appear to be, and no matter how much the person wants us to take charge of his or her life, Invitational

People are able, valuable, and responsible and should be treated accordingly.

Learning is firm: Each individual is responsible for his or her own life. People are able, valuable, and responsible and should be treated accordingly. Only when we accept people as they are, recognize their relatively boundless potential for development, and invite them to make appropriate and caring decisions regarding their present and future, do we contribute to their well-being.

Respect also involves knowing when to invite and when not to invite, when to accept and when not to accept. Sometimes the most inviting thing we can do is not to invite, or not to accept. Offering a cigarette to a friend who is trying to quit smoking, doing things for people that they could and should do for themselves, giving unsolicited advice, saying "yes" when you want to say "no," are all examples of lack of respect. Invitational Learning is far more than the process of sprinkling invitations about like some modern Johnny Appleseed; it involves a dispositional stance regarding ourselves, others, and the world.

Developing respect in human relationships is dependent on an attitudinal quality manifested in a dependable and consistent pattern of action. This pattern of behavior (which we refer to as "stance") creates an environment where respect is cultivated. A respectful stance means that when we offer something beneficial for consideration, we accept the condition that the process of inviting is fluid, and that the needs and wishes of those whom we seek to serve are just as important as our own needs and wishes.

Trust

...professional helping should be a collaborative, cooperative activity where process is as important as product.

Trust is the second vital quality in Invitational Learning. It recognizes the interdependence of human beings and emphasizes that professional helping should be a collaborative, cooperative activity where process is as important as product. Attempting to get others to do what we want them to do without involving them in the process is like beating on cold iron. Even if the effort to control people without their collaboration is successful, the energy expended is usually disproportionate to what is accomplished. As John Dewey explained a half century ago, it is absurd to suppose a person gets more intellectual or mental discipline when he or she goes at a matter unwillingly than when he or she goes at it out of fullness of heart. Trust is enhanced when we give high priority to optimal human welfare, when we view places, policies, programs and processes as contributing to or subtracting from this welfare, and when we recognize that working for the benefit of everyone is the best way to ensure our own welfare.

Trust is seldom won by a single inviting act. Rather, it is dependent on particular ideas that are manifested in an inviting pattern of actions. One difference between Invitational Learning and other approaches to professional helping is that some others require that a trustful relationship be established before any progress can be made. Invitational Learning, by contrast, begins with the desire to help, a willingness to "be with" others, a deliberate preparation of all conditions needed to establish trust, and a genuine response to the concerns of those involved. These attitudes, conditions, and characteristics set the stage for trust to develop. It is through a caring, purposeful, and active commitment that trust is established and maintained.

The condition of establishing trust is observed most clearly when counselors work with clients who have violated the trust of others, or who have had their trust violated, for example, individuals who have committed crimes and are incarcerated, or individuals who have been abused by others. Building trust with such individuals is done over time as a result of the caring and dependable behaviors of counselors demonstrated in the helping relationship.

...working for the benefit of everyone is the best way to ensure our own welfare.

Optimism

A third assumption of Invitational Learning is that people possess relatively untapped potential in all areas of human endeavor. Human capacity is infinite. The uniqueness of human beings is that we have yet to discover any limits on our development.

Optimism is so fundamental to successful functioning that no other assumptions of Invitational Learning could be seriously considered if optimism did not exist. In any helping relationship some level of hope and aspiration is essential. No one, not a child, student, parent, worker, patient, client, teacher, manager, or whoever, can choose a beneficial direction in life without hope that change for the better is possible. Counselors who work with clients, educators who teach students, coaches who train athletes,

The uniqueness of human beings is that we have yet to discover any limits on our development.

nurses who care for patients, parole officers who supervise parolees, and ministers who lead congregations are successful to the degree that they convey an optimistic belief in the value and capabilities of themselves and their fellow human beings.

From an invitational learning point of view, the single most important thing for anyone who joins in a helping relationship is to have a dream, a vision of what it is possible for people to be: To look at a non-reader and see a reader, to look at a non-athlete and see an athelete, to look at someone who seems unable to handle his or her problems and see someone who can. When professional helpers advance optimistically in the direction of their dreams, success is far more likely to be realized.

A corollary of optimism is the belief that everything counts. Nothing in human relations is wasted. No person, place, policy, program, or process can be absolutely neutral. Everything we do, and every way we do it, is either positive or negative, helpful or harmful, inviting or disinviting. In Invitational Learning whatever happens, and whatever way it happens, adds to or takes away from the quality of present existence and future potential. Each experience, no matter how small or in what area, has limitless potential to influence the course of human events. We create ourselves, others, and the places, policies, programs, and processes that make up our world.

Embracing the belief that people possess untapped potential in all areas of human endeavor influences the curricula we devise, the policies we establish, the programs we sponsor, the processes we encourage, and the physical environments we create. As one high school student wrote: "Mr. Penn invited us to like ourselves and to take pride in our work. He expected a great deal of us and we did not let him down. He thought we were brighter than we were, so we were." Optimism, as exhibited by Mr. Penn, is the belief that human potential, though not always apparent, is always there, waiting to be discovered and invited forth.

...the single most important thing for anyone who joins in a helping relationship is to have a dream....

...human potential, though not always apparent, is always there, waiting to be discovered and invited forth.

Intentionality

An invitation can be defined as an **intentional** act designed to offer something beneficial for consideration. The importance of intentionality in helping relationships was first introduced by Rollo May in *Love and Will* (1969). May presented intentionality as a major variable related to successful therapy. He proposed that intentionality is the basis for client intentions and provides the structure by which human perceptions are organized and interpreted. This structure gives meaning to experience. May viewed intentionality as the ability people have to link their perceptions with their overt behaviors. In this sense, he wrote that intentionality "is not to be identified with intentions, but it is the dimension which underlies them; it is man's capacity to have intentions" (1969, p. 224). Intentionality enables helping professionals to create and maintain consistently caring and appropriate relationships characterized by purpose and direction.

...intentionality is a crucial element in any helping relationship.

Invitational Learning proposes that intentionality is a crucial element in any helping relationship. It views intentionality as a bipolar construct that includes both positive and negative intentions. It is possible to be intentionally lethal as well as intentionally beneficial. (In the Broadway play *Amadeus* it is Salieri who uses his special knowledge and great skill to destroy Amadeus Mozart). There is also room between these two poles of intentionally inviting and intentionally disinviting behaviors for behaviors that are purposeless, careless, thoughtless, or accidental. Such behaviors, while **unintentional**, can be profoundly helpful or harmful in their outcomes. Counselors, teachers, coaches, ministers, psychologists, nurses, and allied professionals have the knowledge and skills to offer vital service to others, or to do significant damage. Helpers can be a beneficial presence, or a lethal one, in their own lives and in the lives of those they serve. An awareness of the helpful or harmful potential of every intentional and unintentional action is a major responsibility in Invitational Learning.

Helpers can be a beneficial presence, or a lethal one, in their own lives and in the lives of those they serve.

At a practical level, the more intentional we are, the more we are able to "hold the point." Champion bird dogs are judged in part by how long and how well they can "hold the point" when they detect a covey of birds. Similarly, those of us who employ Invitational Learning are best judged by the ways we consistently and dependably invite well-being in ourselves and others, personally and professionally.

An example of the importance of intentionality was provided by one of the authors' daughter, Cynthia Purkey

Norton. Cynthia graduated from college in mid-year and accepted a mid-year teaching appointment in an inner city elementary school. Unfortunately, the class she inherited had lost several teachers during the first part of the year. The result was that the class had become very difficult to manage. Cynthia struggled, with only mixed success, to apply Invitational Learning in her classroom. While most of the students responded well, one unkempt, overweight, unhappy and sullen little girl (we will call her Sarah) showed absolutely no improvement. Sarah continued to cause trouble and took great vocal offense at the slightest perceived affront. Cynthia tried hard, but her frequent lament was: "Dad, Invitational Learning is not working with Sarah!" Dad continued to urge her to "hold her point," that it took a long time for Sarah to get where she is, and that it will take time for her to change. The payoff came on the final day of school. Sarah arrived with a special gift she had laboriously made and inscribed to her "Favorite Teacher." They shared a big hug and a few tears.

As Peck noted in *The Road Less Traveled* (1978) "the person who truly loves does so because of a decision to love" (p. 119). It takes intentionality to consistently and dependably offer something beneficial for consideration, particularly in the face of apparent rejection.

The four essential elements of Invitational Learning offer professionals a consistent "stance" through which they can create personal and professional relationships that encourage the realization of human potential. While there are other elements that contribute to beneficial relationships, these four, **respect, trust, optimism,** and **intentionality** are the key forces in Invitational Learning. Chapter 2 offers a detailed look at the foundations of Invitational Learning: The Perceptual Tradition and Self-Concept Theory.

Chapter 2

Foundations of Invitational Learning

For men and women are not only themselves; they are also the region in which they were born, the city apartment or the farm in which they learned to walk, the games they played as children, the old wives' tale they overheard, the food they ate, the schools they attended, the sports they followed, the poems they read, and the god they believed in.

The Razor's Edge
—W. Somerset Maugham

Invitational Learning springs from the fountainheads of two theoretical perspectives: the perceptual tradition and self-concept theory. This chapter presents a brief overview of these two perspectives as they form successive foundations for Invitational Learning.

Invitational Learning springs from...two theoretical perspectives: the perceptual tradition and self-concept theory.

The Perceptual Tradition

The perceptual tradition in understanding human behavior and potential consists of all those systems of thought in which efforts are made to view humans as they typically and normally view themselves. The term **perceptual** refers not only to the senses but also the meanings—the personal significance of an event for the individual experiencing it. These meanings extend far beyond sensory receptors to include all such personal experiences as feelings, desires, aspirations, and the ways people view themselves, others, the world, and their relationships with these phenomena.

The perceptual tradition is in contrast to other theoretical viewpoints such as classical behaviorism or Freudianism. Behaviorism depicts behavior as a complex bundle of stimuli and responses, while Freudianism views our actions as the product of unconscious urges and repressed desires. In the perceptual tradition, primary importance is given to each person's perceived world, rather than to objective behavior or unconscious processes.

Since the perceptual tradition maintains that everyone behaves in terms of how they see things, healthy human development is enhanced when individuals understand the nature of their perceptions. As explained by Combs, Avila, and Purkey (1978):

> Human behavior is always a product of how people see themselves and the situations in which they are involved. Although this fact seems obvious, the failure of people everywhere to comprehend it is responsible for much of human misunderstanding, maladjustment, conflict, and loneliness. Our perceptions of ourselves and the world are so real that we seldom pause to doubt them. Since persons behave in terms of their personal perceptions, effective helping must start with the helper's understanding of the nature and dynamics of perceiving. (p. 15)

By accepting the basic assumption of the perceptual tradition, that people behave according to their perceptions, professional helpers can seek to "read behavior backwards," to infer from behavior the perceptual worlds of the behaving person.

An example of how important it is to understand things from the internal point of view was provided by a first grade teacher. She said that she had the habit of squatting down when talking with young children so she could approach them at their eye level. One day the teacher squatted down to chat with a group of kindergartners. Suddenly, as if by magic, the children squatted down too. When looked at from the internal vantage point of the children, their actions make perfect sense: The teacher's behavior was perceived by the children as an invitation to squat!

The perceptual tradition has special value for professional helpers who employ Invitational Learning because it gives primary consideration to the belief systems of helpers.

Our perceptions of ourselves and the world are so real that we seldom pause to doubt them.

The perceptual tradition...gives primary consideration to the belief systems of helpers.

No single explanation, of course, can cover the entire phenomenon of professional success or failure. However, it is becoming increasingly clear that the belief systems of the helper, in addition to determining his or her behavior, have great power in influencing how students, clients, or patients view themselves and their abilities. This determines their behavior as well. As Jourard (1968) explained: "The teacher who turns on the dull student, the coach who elicits a magnificent performance from someone of whom it could not be expected, are people who **themselves** have an image of the pupils' possibilities; and they were effective in realizing their images" (p. 126). Like a master sculptor who envisions something in a block of marble that others cannot see, professional helpers with an Invitational Learning perspective see possibilities in individuals that others may miss.

Studies that have focused most clearly on the perceptions and belief systems of professional helpers are those of Combs (1972); Combs, Avila and Purkey (1971, 1978); Combs and Soper (1963a, 1963b); Combs et al. (1969); and O'Roark (1974). In a series of investigations extending for more than a decade, Combs and associates studied the ways in which successful helpers organize their perceptions of themselves, others, and the world. The researchers also investigated the ways in which these perceptual organizations influence effectiveness in helping others. Combs et al. (1969) reported that effective helpers in many professions, including teaching, counseling, nursing, the ministry, administration, and public service could be distinguished from less effective helpers on the basis of their perceptual worlds. The researchers concluded that a high degree of similarity exists among the perceptions of "good" helpers in various fields. Good teachers, for example, can be clearly identified from poor ones on the basis of their perceptions of themselves, others, and the world. They tend to see people as able rather than unable, friendly rather than unfriendly, worthy rather than unworthy, dependable rather than undependable, helpful rather than hindering, and internally, rather than externally motivated. From these studies there seems to be sufficient support for two major assumptions of Invitational Learning. First, how professional helpers view themselves, others, and the world largely determines how well they function. Second, the ways in which professional helpers function play a major role in determining the

...how professional helpers view themselves, others, and the world largely determines how well they function.

perceptions and eventually the behavior of their clients, students, or patients.

Helpers who use Invitational Learning in their personal and professional lives understand that an individual's behavior may make little or no sense when observed externally, but becomes logical and understandable when seen from the internal viewpoint of the perceiving individual. These helpers also realize that of all the perceptions we have in life, none is more instrumental in our success or failure than the perceptions we have of ourselves. It is the sum total of these self-perceptions that gives us the second foundation of Invitational Learning: self-concept theory.

Self-Concept Theory

The search for personal identity and significance in the face of continuous internal and external pressures appears to be a basic human concern. Some theorists (Combs, Avila & Purkey, 1971, 1978; Rogers, 1951, 1967; Purkey & Schmidt, 1987) have postulated that the maintenance and enhancement of the **perceived self** (one's own personal existence as viewed internally) are the motives behind all human behavior. Use of this postulate, embedded within what is generally known as **self-concept theory**, can clarify and help us understand behavior.

...the maintenance and enhancement of the perceived self...are the motives behind all human behavior.

The following story by a colleague who refuses to sing illustrates the long-term impact of a negative self-concept.

> I can remember when I was in elementary school our class was invited to sing before the PTA. The teacher wanted very much for us to do our best (the superintendent would be in the audience) so she had each child audition. When my turn came to audition, the teacher listened and then said: 'Rosemary, I'd rather you not sing. You just stand in the back row and move your mouth.' I stood in the back row at the performance, moved my mouth, and tears rolled down my cheeks. I have never uttered a note in public from that day to this.

Once a self-concept is formed, in this case a negative view of oneself as a singer, it guides all future behavior.

It is helpful to pause here and define self-concept as a learned, organized, and active system of subjective beliefs that an individual holds to be true regarding his or her own personal existence. It serves to guide behavior and enables each individual to assume particular roles in life. Rather than initiating activity, self-concept serves as a perceptual filter and guides the direction of behavior. For example, self-concept does not cause a client to become dysfunctional. A better explanation is that the person has learned to see oneself as unable, worthless, and irresponsible and behaves accordingly. When individuals have doubts about their identity as able, valuable, and responsible persons, they are likely to engage in various self-defeating behaviors. As documented by Suls and Greenwald (1983) depressive disorders are the result of defective self-schemas. In other words, self-concept is a moderator variable. It influences the direction behavior takes.

> *...self-concept*
> *...a learned,*
> *organized, and*
> *active system of*
> *subjective beliefs*
> *that an individual*
> *holds to be true*
> *regarding his or*
> *her own personal*
> *existence.*

Basic Assumptions of Self-Concept

Self-concept has at least three major qualities of importance to professional helpers: (1) it is learned, (2) it is dynamic and (3) it is organized. Each of these qualities, with corollaries, was presented in an ERIC/CAPS Digest *An Overview of Self-Concept Theory for Counselors* (Purkey, 1989).

Self-concept is learned. As far as we know, no one is born with a self-concept. Self-awareness gradually emerges in the early months of life and is shaped and reshaped through repeated perceived experiences, particularly with significant others. A student wrote:

> In my junior year of high school, my favorite teacher and I engaged in a discussion about the girls and boys most likely to be nominated for student council president. I named two of the class leaders as most likely to be chosen. She agreed that they were both highly qualified, but then she asked, "And what about you?" I remember thinking that this was hilarious—I had never been elected to anything in my life. Still, the teacher insisted that I had leadership qualities. Much later, she told me that she was not a bit surprised when I was nominated and elected as student council president.

Successful helpers are magic mirrors, reflecting back the message that people are able, valuable, and capable....

Successful helpers are magic mirrors, reflecting back the message that people are able, valuable, and capable and should behave accordingly.

The fact that self-concept is learned has some important implications:

- Because self-concept is a social product, developed through repeated experiences, it possesses relatively boundless potential for development and actualization.
- Individuals perceive different aspects of themselves at different times with varying degrees of clarity.
- Any experience which is inconsistent with one's self-concept may be perceived as a threat, and the more of these experiences there are, the more rigid the self-concept becomes to maintain and protect itself.
- Individuals strive to behave in ways that are in keeping with their self-concepts, no matter how helpful or harmful to oneself or others.
- Self-concept usually takes precedence over the physical body. Individuals will often sacrifice physical comfort and safety for self-concept reasons.
- Self-concept continuously guards itself against loss of self-esteem, for it is this loss that produces feelings of anxiety and worthlessness.

Because the self-concept is so profound in its influence, professional helpers who ignore this internal gyrocompass would be like automobile mechanics who ignore steering systems.

The most influential and eloquent voice in self-concept theory was that of Carl Rogers who introduced an entire system of professional helping built around the development of self-concept. In Rogers' view, self-concept is the central ingredient in human personality and personal adjustment. Rogers described the self-concept as a social product, developing out of interpersonal relationships and striving for stability and consistency. He maintained that there is a basic human need for positive regard both from oneself and from others. He also believed that in every person there is a tendency toward self-actualization and development as long as this is permitted and encouraged by an inviting

...there is a basic human need for positive regard both from oneself and from others.

environment. An example of how self-concept guides behavior was provided by an outstanding student athlete:

> In elementary school, I was told by my classmates "any girl can kick better than you." I was always picked last for kickball teams because I could not kick the ball into the air (a firm rule was no grounders). On one particular day my teacher, who was sitting with another teacher watching the kick-ball game, saw me kick another grounder. This lady (all six feet of her) called me aside and showed me how to kick under the ball. When I got to kick, the ball sailed in the air. I'll always remember that teacher who took the time to show me that I could succeed in athletics. I have adored athletics ever since.

Any successful experience, in any area, has boundless potential.

In concluding this section on the learned nature of self-concept, it is important to remind ourselves that one of the probable reasons for the apparent failure of many programs designed to "enhance," "build," or "modify" self-concept is the tendency to overlook the conservative nature of the self. Whether a self-perception is psychologically healthy or unhealthy, beneficial or lethal, people cling to their learned self-perceptions, as a drowning person clings to a straw, and act accordingly. It took a long time for people to get where they are, it will take time for them to change. As we explained earlier, it is important for helpers to "hold their point."

...people cling to their learned self-perceptions, as a drowning person clings to a straw, and act accordingly.

Self-concept is dynamic. To understand the dynamic nature of self-concept, it helps to imagine it as a gyro-compass: A continuously active system that dependably points to the "true north" of a person's perceived existence. The role of self-concept is to provide a stabilizing rudder for the human personality. Without this rudder, the personality would have no protection against environmental forces that push the person here and there. This internal guidance system not only shapes the ways a person views oneself, others and the world, but also serves to direct actions and enables each person to take and maintain a consistent "stance" in life. The dynamic quality of self-concept carries corollaries.

- The world and the things in it are not just perceived; they are always perceived in relation to one's self-concept. There can be no "out there" without an "in here."
- Self-concept development is a continuous process. In the healthy personality there is constant assimilation of new ideas and expulsion of old ideas throughout the life span.
- Faulty thinking patterns, such as dichotomous reasoning (dividing everything in terms of opposites or extremes) or overgeneralizing (making sweeping conclusions based on little information) function in ways that contribute to negative self-concepts.

Fortunately, because self-concept is learned, it can be taught.

There is growing awareness on the part of both the public and professionals that the dynamic nature of self-concept cannot be ignored if we are to successfully address such nagging problems as drug and alcohol abuse, dropout rates, dysfunctional families, crime and violence, child abuse, teenage pregnancy, prostitution, chronic welfare dependency, and failure of children to succeed in school. Helping professionals in a multitude of settings are challenged by the task of bringing the home, school, church, civic clubs and a myriad of other organizations together to focus on self-concept development.

Self-concept is organized. Most researchers agree that self-concept has a stable quality that is characterized by orderliness and harmony. Each person maintains countless perceptions regarding one's personal existence, and each perception is orchestrated with all the others. It is this generally stable and organized quality that gives consistency to the human personality. This organized quality of self-concept also has corollaries.

Each person maintains countless perceptions regarding one's personal existence, and each perception is orchestrated with all the others.

- Self-concept requires consistency, stability, and tends to resist change. In fact, if self-concept changed readily, the individual would lack a consistent and dependable personality.
- The more central a particular belief is in one's self-concept, the more resistant one is to changing that belief.

- At the heart of self-concept is the self-as-doer, the "I," which is distinct from the self-as-object, the various "me's." This allows the person to reflect on past events, analyze present perceptions, and shape future experiences.
- Because basic perceptions of oneself are quite stable, change takes time. A vital attribute of any professional helper is patience.
- Perceived success and failure impact heavily on self-concept. Failure in a highly regarded area lowers evaluations in all other areas as well. Success in a prized area raises evaluation in other seemingly unrelated areas.

The tendency toward internal organization appears to be a necessary feature of human personality. It provides the individual's entire being with internal balance, a sense of direction, and a feeling of stability. If individuals adopted new beliefs about themselves rapidly, or if their behavior was capricious, human progress would be difficult to imagine. Fortunately, the great majority of us are remarkably consistent in our self-concepts.

If individuals adopted new beliefs about themselves rapidly,…human progress would be difficult to imagine.

Being aware of the basic qualities of self-concept (that it is **learned**, **dynamic**, and **organized**), and the contributions of the perceptual tradition are fundamental to Invitational Learning. With these understandings, professional helpers can gain a deeper appreciation of the importance of the people, places, policies, programs and processes in life that shape these perceptions—for good or ill.

Invitational Learning takes the position that the most logical way to positively influence self-concept development is to explore and improve the myriad messages, formal and informal, witting and unwitting, that invite people to feel able, valuable, and responsible, and to reduce or eliminate those messages that inform them that they are unable, worthless, and irresponsible. In Invitational Learning, these positive and negative messages are categorized into four major levels of personal and professional functioning. These levels are presented in Chapter 3.

Chapter 3

Four Levels of Functioning

Now, one person can invite another to change his being in many ways. I can invite you to change the meanings you attach to things and events, to reconstrue your world. I can invite you to change from the inauthentic way to the authentic way. I can invite you to buy and sell. It follows that I can invite you to try living in new ways when you have experienced yourself as invited to die. When your purposes have worn out, when it seems that there is no place for you and your way of being a person in a given time and place, and when you feel you have already been abandoned by others, I can invite you to reinvent yourself and find challenge in new projects.

The Transparent Self
—Sidney Jourard

In addition to centering itself on the four elements of **respect, trust, optimism**, and **intentionality**, and building on the foundations of the perceptual tradition and self-concept theory, Invitational Learning identifies four levels of functioning. All of us function at each of these four levels from time to time, but it is the level at which we typically function that determines our approach to life and our success in our personal and professional lives.

It is helpful to pause here and contemplate the complexity of Invitational Learning. Some helpers may think they already understand "inviting." They believe it is simply doing nice things for people—sharing a smile, giving a hug, or buying a gift. But Invitational Learning is far more than "warm fuzzies," "strokes," "hug stations" or walking around with IALAC sheets. While these are worthwhile activities when used caringly and appropriately, they are only manifestations of a theoretical stance one takes. The stance one selects will determine the level of personal and professional functioning. We have identified four of these levels, plus a "plus factor."

Intentionally Disinviting

The most toxic and lethal level of human functioning involves those actions, places, policies, programs and processes that are deliberately designed to dissuade, discourage, defeat, demean, and destroy. Examples of **Level One** functioning might be a sales clerk who is deliberately insulting, a hospital policy that is intentionally discriminatory, a prison program that willfully demeans inmates, or an environment made purposefully unpleasant and unattractive. For example, after attending a workshop on Invitational Learning, a teacher sent a note to the principal pointing out that the girl's bathroom needed soap, paper towels and tissue. Her note was returned to her mailbox at the end of the day with this remark written across the bottom (unsigned) "What do you think this place is—the Hilton?" With such an intentionally disinviting attitude, is it any wonder that students in this particular school are so apathetic or unruly, or that the school has the reputation of being one of the worst in the state?

Fortunately, there are very few individuals who, like Elvira Gulch in the 1939 film version of L. Frank Baum's *Wizard of Oz*, take special pleasure in hurting people and seeing them upset ("I'll get you, my Pretty, and your little dog too!"). Individuals in the helping professions whose stance is based primarily on pessimism, contempt, and suspicion, and whose level of functioning is intentionally disinviting are rare. Their intentional signals to themselves and others that they are unworthy, incapable, and irresponsible may be understandable, and forgivable, but never justifiable. In Invitational Learning, intentionally disinviting people, places, policies, programs and processes cannot be justified regardless of effectiveness, efficiency, or any apparent success they might bring. Again, the ends do not justify the means. In Invitational Learning, there can be no justification for people, places, policies, programs, or processes to be, or to remain, at this bottom level of functioning.

It may seem contradictory that a helping professional could function at the intentionally disinviting level, but it does happen. We believe that there are at least two reasons why professionals might choose to operate in this lethal manner. The first happens when a professional helper becomes upset and frustrated by circumstances and makes decisions based on these feelings. In applying Invitational Learning, it helps to keep the **HALT** concept in mind: never make important decisions when you are Hungry, Angry, Lonely, or Tired. (The importance of being inviting with oneself as a first step in being inviting with others will be emphasized later in this monograph).

A second way that professional helpers operate at the intentionally disinviting level is when they use their professional relationships to behave in unethical, immoral, and illegal ways. Racial or sexual prejudices, illicit use of mind-altering materials, dishonest business transactions, improper sexual relations or sexual harassments are a few examples of this lowest level of functioning.

Being human, all helpers will slip dangerously close to the intentionally disinviting level from time to time. Daily frustrations, difficulties, and apparent inability to cope affect all of us in negative ways. An extreme example of intentionally disinviting behavior by a teacher was reported by a graduate student describing an incident that happened when she was in elementary school:

Being human, all helpers will slip dangerously close to the intentionally disinviting level from time to time.

> When I was in kindergarten, Mrs. Hall made me sit beside Illmar. No one wanted to sit next to him because he smelled bad and always had a runny nose. One day he bit me on the arm. I told Mrs. Hall and she said if he did it again he would have to move. So JoLynn (my friend) said she would bite my arm (teeth marks for proof) and I could tell Mrs. Hall. When I showed Mrs. Hall my arm she became furious. She asked me if I wanted to bite Illmar back. Of course I didn't, so the teacher bit him on the arm.

Intentionally disinviting behavior is sometimes justified as "being good for them," "getting their attention," "the only language they understand," "fighting fire with fire," "an object lesson," and the like. As this monograph is being

...we can think of no circumstances in which a professional can justify intentionally disinviting behavior.

written, the United States Government is considering "boot camps" on military bases for drug offenders—concentration camps designed to teach them a lesson. From our understanding of the effects of such actions, the lessons taught will not be the ones intended. Moreover, we can think of no circumstances in which a professional can justify intentionally disinviting behavior. Laws are necessary and penalties unavoidable. But even under the worst of circumstances, the accused and convicted person deserves to be treated with respect. A vast difference exists between a state trooper and a storm trooper.

If intentionally disinviting people, programs, policies, processes, and places go unchallenged, then the very institutions established by society—schools, hospitals, rest homes, reformatories, treatment centers, clinics, and other agencies along with the people who work there—move away from their primary function which is to create and maintain a beneficial relationship with those they seek to serve.

Unintentionally Disinviting

People, places, policies, programs, and processes that are intentionally disinviting are few in number compared to those that are unintentionally disinviting. Unfortunately, it often happens that well-meaning, high-minded professionals with the best of intentions function at **Level Two**, as the following episode attests:

> When I was in junior high school I had a great desire to join the school band. When the band met that first afternoon I remember how nervous I was. I told the band director I wanted to play the drums. She laughed and said "Little girls aren't allowed to play the drums." Then she turned to the other students and said: "This little girl wants to play the drums" and the students laughed. The teacher said I was to play the flute and a little part of me died. I tried playing the flute for a few months, and hated every minute of it. I quit the band and I've never learned to play a musical instrument.

Unintentionally disinviting actions are usually the result of a lack of stance. Because there is no philosophy of **respect, trust, optimism,** and **intentionality,** behaviors are exhibited, policies established, programs designed, places arranged, and processes instituted that are clearly disinviting although such was not the intent.

Professionals who function at **Level Two** spend a great deal of time wondering "Why are things not going as well as I would like?" "Why can't people take a joke?" "Why are people upset with me?" "Why did the client drop his appointments with me?" "Why are my students not learning more?" In most cases when people function at the unintentionally disinviting level they do so because they are careless, thoughtless, or both. Like the band director, they do not intend to be hurtful and harmful, but because they lack consistency in direction and purpose they behave in unintentionally disinviting ways.

Professionals who typically function at **Level Two** are often viewed as uncaring, chauvinistic, condescending, patronizing, sexist, racist, dictatorial, or just plain thoughtless. Examples of **Level Two** can be found everywhere: The committee chairperson who always asks a female to take minutes, the school sign that reads NO STUDENTS ALLOWED, the clinic policy of reserving the best parking places for staff, the refusal of an agency to accept checks, the act of pushing papers at one's desk while someone is waiting at the door to speak, or the impoliteness of drinking coffee during a counseling session without offering the client a cup. Those who function at **Level Two** do not intend to be disinviting, but the damage is done. It's like being hit by a truck; intended or not, you are still dead.

Unintentionally disinviting forces can also be seen at work in the ways people describe themselves and their abilities in the most negative terms: "I'm such a klutz," "I have a tin ear," "I have two left feet," "I'm all thumbs," "I can't carry a tune in a bucket," "I eat like a horse," "I never know what to say." If anyone else described them in such unflattering ways they would be highly insulted. Sadly, they are usually unaware that they have the habit of referring to themselves in such negative terms. They have unintentionally joined the ranks of their own enemies.

Unintentionally Inviting

Professionals who typically function at Level Three have stumbled serendipitously into ways of functioning that are often effective.

Professionals who typically function at **Level Three** have stumbled serendipitously into ways of functioning that are often effective. However, when asked to explain their philosophy they have difficulty. Because they lack a consistent stance, they can usually describe **what** they do, but not **why**. Occasionally, they are not even sure what they have done that results in beneficial outcomes. Helpers who perform at **Level Three** can be imagined as the "natural born" professional. They are often successful in their roles because they exhibit many of the respecting, trusting, and optimistic qualities associated with Invitational Learning. However, because they lack the fourth critical element, **intentionality**, they lack consistency and dependability in their actions and the policies, programs, places, and processes they create and maintain.

Beginning counselors sometimes fall into a **Level Three** mode of functioning because they have not had time to develop a consistent stance. They are successful in the beginning stages of assisting clients but encounter growing difficulties as they move deeper into the counseling relationship. For example, a counselor may be seen as caring and understanding by a client, but after several sessions the client stops coming. It is not that the client is upset with the counselor but that he or she feels that the counseling sessions are not going anywhere. To "go somewhere" a relationship requires intentionality in direction and purpose.

Young teachers sometimes fall into a similar trap. While they are likeable, entertaining, enthusiastic, funny, and graduated just in time to save education, they lack intentionality regarding their goals. As a colleague John Novak pointed out, the process of Invitational Learning involves not only encounters with students in positive and caring ways, but also a teacher's personal relationship with the content and essence of what he or she teaches. A teacher who perceives meaning, clarity, and significance in what he or she teaches is better able to invite students to do likewise.

A teacher who perceives meaning, clarity, and significance in what he or she teaches is better able to invite students to do likewise.

Those who operate at **Level Three** are somewhat like the early barnstorming airplane pilots. These pioneer pilots did not know much about aerodynamics, weather patterns, or navigational systems. As long as they stayed close to the ground, followed a road or railway track, and the weather was clear, they were able to function. But when they flew above cloud cover, the weather turned bad, or night fell, they might quickly become disoriented and lost. In difficult situations those at **Level Three** lack consistency in direction and dependability in behavior.

Professionals functioning at **Level Three** are also vulnerable. Because they have little or no understanding of the principles involved in Invitational Learning, when faced with threatening situations or challenges, they may drop to **Level Two** (unintentionally disinviting) or even **Level One** (intentionally disinviting). A case in point was described by a high school counselor:

> In my first year as a high school counselor I wanted to be well liked by my kids. I kidded, joked around, and tried to be one of the gang. Gradually things got out of hand. The students, while they liked me, became overly familiar, called me by my first name, pulled little tricks on me, and the like. One day I was walking down the corridor and a high school girl, standing by her locker, suddenly slapped my bottom. It was a spontaneous sort of thing. On being hit I swirled around and said in an angry voice: "Keep your hands to yourself!" The girl looked at me first with astonishment, then deep hurt, and ran down the hallway crying. My unintentionally inviting behavior had led me to an intentionally disinviting act.

The basic weakness in functioning at the unintentionally inviting level is the inability to identify the reasons for successes or failures. We know something is, or is not, working but we are unable to tell what "it" is. If whatever "it" is stops working, we are puzzled about how to start "it" up again. Those who function at **Level Three** lack a consistent stance—a dependable position from which to operate. Invitational Learning requires that we create and maintain a consistently inviting stance, even in the rain, which brings us to **Level Four**.

Intentionally Inviting

From an Invitational Learning viewpoint, the best way to place oneself in the path of success is to be intentionally inviting with oneself and others, personally and professionally.

When professional helpers function at **Level Four**, they exhibit the essential elements of **respect**, **trust**, **optimism**, and **intentionality**. In addition, they work to practice their professional talents with a high degree of fluency. Functioning at this high level requires a clear understanding of one's abilities. An awareness of one's skills allows for appropriate and caring decisions to be made about strategies and techniques to be used.

At times, human service is so fluent that the skills involved are invisible. It is similar to comparing a beginning art student who is just learning to hold a brush to a master artist at the peak of her career. The artist paints with such talented assurance that the art does not call attention to itself. In like manner, Invitational Learning at its best becomes invisible, as we will soon explain.

While skills and knowledge are essential, it is the way that they are combined with philosophy that determines success or failure. Gilbert Wrenn (1973) summed up this concept when he wrote: "To me the most striking personal discovery of the past decade has been that people respond to my degree of caring more than to my degree of knowing" (pp. 248-249). A beautiful example of **Level Four** commitment is presented by Mizer (1964), who described how schools can function to turn a child "into a zero." Mizer illustrated the tragedy of one such child, then concluded her article with these words:

> I look up and down the rows carefully each September at the unfamiliar faces. I look for veiled eyes or bodies scrounged into an alien world. "Look, Kids," I say silently, "I may not do anything else for you this year, but not one of you is going to come out of here a nobody. I'll work or fight to the bitter end doing battle with society and the school board, but I won't have one of you coming out of here thinking of himself as a zero." (p. 10)

Being clear in our own minds about our intentionality can be a tremendous asset....

Being clear in our own minds about our intentionality can be a tremendous asset, for it serves to remind us of the truly important parts of the educative process.

In Invitational Learning, **everybody** and **everything** adds to, or subtracts from, the realization of human potential. Ideally, the factors of people, places, policies, programs and processes should be so intentionally inviting as to create a world where each individual is cordially summoned to develop physically, intellectually, psychologically, and spiritually. With this in mind, **Level Four** is the heart of Invitational Learning. The more intentionally inviting something is, the more its lends itself to understanding, consistency, direction, and evaluation. Recognizing the importance and accepting the responsibility of being intentionally inviting can be a tremendous asset for professional helpers. Those of us who accept the principles of Invitational Learning not only strive to reach **Level Four**, but once there continue to grow and develop. This brings us to the "Plus Factor."

The Plus Factor

When you watch the master teacher, the skilled counselor, the artfully inviting minister, the world class athlete, the accomplished musician, what he or she does seems simple. It is only when you try to do it yourself that you realize true art requires painstaking care, discipline and planning. Moreover, it does not call attention to itself. For example, manners are an acquired amenity but the goal of good manners is to have them so ingrained that they appear to be innate.

At its best, Invitational Learning becomes "invisible" because it has become a means of addressing humanity. To borrow the words of Chuang-tse, an ancient Chinese Philosopher, "it flows like water, reflects like a mirror, and responds like an echo." The spirit of Invitational Learning requires implicit rather than explicit expression. When the professional reaches this special plateau of Invitational Learning, what he or she does appears effortless. World class athletes call it "finding the zone," fighter pilots call it "rhythm," we call it the "**Plus Factor**."

Making Invitational Learning look easy is what makes it so hard. When Ginger Rogers described dancing with Fred Astaire she said, "It's a lot of hard work, that I do know." Someone responded: "But it doesn't look it, Ginger." Ginger replied "That's why it's magic." Invitational Learning, at its best, works like magic.

Finding the **Plus Factor** means to develop the ability to approach the most difficult situations in a professionally

At its best, Invitational Learning becomes "invisible" because it has become a means of addressing humanity.

inviting manner. When professional helpers who are functioning at this advanced level face challenges, they are able to rely on their understanding of Invitational Learning and develop solutions. Thanks to their stance, they can "fly on instruments" around or over dangerous weather. In the words of one colleague, they can "Invite, even in the rain." Because they have a dependable stance, they can maintain a true course even under the worst of conditions. And after all, it is the rain that causes things to grow.

Recognizing the importance of being intentionally inviting and striving to use this ability in the most artful manner can be tremendous assets in helping. By understanding the four levels of functioning, by seeking to transcend upper limits, and by constantly seeking to improve abilities at the highest possible level, professional helpers can assist people to realize their relatively boundless potential. Chapter 4 will introduce the "Five Powerful P's" and explain how each contributes to Invitational Learning.

Chapter 4

The Five Powerful P's

And so the human individual is built. He has a body like no other. It is a remarkable creation, having built into it many automatic, self-regulating devices. It has enormous recuperative powers, and will stand unconscionable abuse, showing the enormous will to live which we observe in all living things. It feeds on physical things, although these are selectively chosen by each individual and are not the same for any two persons except where there is only one thing to be had. He has a unique psychological self which controls his behavior. This is built out of the perceptive stuff of growth, also selected in keeping with his unique experience and purpose. The food of this self consists of whatever there is around him to select from —squalor, rejection, hostility, love, beauty, sunsets, symphonies. All of these things, physical and perceptual, are what the individual is, and provide the basis for our consideration of individuality.

Another Look at Individualism
—Earl Kelly

An organization is like a big bowl of jello—you poke it anywhere and the whole thing jiggles. Everything is connected to everything else. In applying Invitational Learning it is important to remember that **everything** counts in inviting individuals to realize their potential. This includes the **places** (hallways, offices, restrooms, waiting rooms, lawns, libraries, classrooms, commons, athletic fields, foyers), the **policies** (rules, codes, guidelines, regulations, statutes, laws, directives), the **programs** (curricular and extracurricular, specialized and unspecialized, restricted and unrestricted), the **processes** (the manner and spirit in which the other "P's" exist), and the **people** (custodians, secretaries, teachers, administrators, nurses, volunteers, families, friends, cafeteria staff, coaches, counselors, crossing guards, supervisors). Again, everything adds to, or subtracts from, the quality of life in organizations. It will help to examine these five powerful "P's" more closely.

The Places

In seeking to change any environment, the easiest place to begin is the physical setting. After all, almost everyone can agree that a hallway is dingy, a bathroom is unpleasant, an office is unattractive, the walkways are littered, a cafeteria is grimy, a classroom dusty. Because physical environments are so obvious in their appearance, they are usually the easiest to change. Moreover, they offer a golden opportunity for **immediate** improvement.

An excellent illustration of how a physical environment can be made inviting is in Orange County, Virginia. The food service professionals in the high school made the cafeteria so clean, well-lighted, stimulating, hospitable, attractive and appealing that several weddings have taken place there!

Everything we do in life is influenced by the physical setting.

Everything we do in life is influenced by the physical setting. Our behaviors at home are colored by the tones and shades of the physcial environment. Our performance at work is enhanced or diminished by the trappings of the office, classroom or other workplace. Our home and job environments are a reflection of the respect, trust, optimism and intentionality of the people who live and work there. For this reason, everything in the physical setting is to be carefully considered when applying Invitational Learning.

Usually an evaluation of physical environments will quickly identify factors that can be altered, adjusted, or improved in some way to create a more inviting place. In the home, it may be as simple as placing a nightlight in childrens' bedrooms to help them go to sleep, or as complex as adding an attractive family room. In the workplace it might mean painting walls, hanging pictures, bringing flowers, planting trees, changing light bulbs, installing new carpeting, cleaning windows, altering signs on doors, or changing bulletin boards. Once the decision is made to improve the place, ways can be found to do it. As Glenda, the Good Witch, reminded Dorothy in the 1939 Hollywood Film *The Wizard of Oz*: "You always had the power, my child, you just didn't want hard enough." Once people **want** to create an inviting physical environment, the environment begins to change.

Once people want to create an inviting physical environment, the environment begins to change.

Visitors to counseling offices, classrooms, and other work areas notice that certain places feel comfortable while others, perhaps just as new and basically well-furnished, feel uncomfortable. For example, one counseling office is arranged to offer maximum privacy so that confidential relationships can be honored, while another is designed with little regard for people and their feelings. The reason for these differences goes back to the perceptual orientation (theoretical stance) of professional helpers described in **Chapter Two.** If professionals recognize the importance of an inviting physical environment, they are likely to take positive action. A pleasant physical environment is a major way that professionals demonstrate their concern for the people they seek to serve.

Schools provide many illustrations of how physical places influence the behavior of people. For example, to encourage good behavior in students one school plays music over the speaker system in the hallways during class changes. If the students can hear the music, they know that their noise level is appropriate. If they can't hear the music, they know they are being too loud. In another school, to improve the reception area of the outer office a junior high school principal decided to strengthen the lighting, add new furniture and carpeting, and remove the tall counter. When the counter disappeared the secretary reported, "I feel I've been let out of prison!"

Improving the physical environment is only the first step, but a very important one. Coaches report that the first rung in the ladder to a winning season is "painting the locker room." The same emphasis on the physical environment as a first step in Invitational Learning, seems valid in all professional settings.

The Policies

The places we create are closely related to the policies we establish and maintain. Policies refer to the guidelines, rules, procedures, codes, directives and so forth that regulate the ongoing functions of organizations and people. Policies are everywhere, issued by governments, boards, parents, administrators, supervisors, directors, executives, governors, wardens, legislators, and commanding officers. Unavoidably, the policies we create, whether they are enforced or unenforced, formal or informal, reasonable or unreasonable, communicate powerful messages of trust or distrust, respect or disrespect, and optimism or pessimism. Whether intended or unintended, policies, like places, reveal the perceptual orientation of the policy makers.

Every organization no matter its size or purpose has a set of rules and regulations, written or unwritten, by which its members function. When policies place unreasonable restrictions on people they detract from the overall potential of the organization, and sometimes contribute to the difficulties of people. In applying Invitational Learning, counselors and other helpers carefully appraise the procedures used in governing institutions and organizations. For example, professional counselors in diverse settings help parents identify family rules that are reasonable for everyone, assist schools with policies that encourage student responsibility and participation rather than demand conformity, and plan hospital admitting procedures that place high regard on the patient and less concern on the convenience of the staff.

Unfortunately, some policies are created that reflect a lack of trust, respect, and optimism.

Unfortunately, some policies are created that reflect a lack of trust, respect, and optimism. Examples might be the rest home policy of lights out at 10:00 p.m., the elementary principal who demands complete silence from children during lunchtime, the counseling center that does not accept personal checks, buses that leave exactly on time regardless of circumstances, or a school directive permitting corporal punishment. Although probably well-intended, policies that are insensitive, uncaring, disrespectful, racist, sexist, or inappropriate have no connection with Invitational Learning.

...policies that are insensitive, uncaring, disrespectful, racist, sexist, or inappropriate have no connection with Invitational Learning.

One highly successful middle school teacher has one policy that covers everything—**respect**. He takes time during the opening days of school to discuss the concept of respect with his students. He reports that this practice frees him from "rule fixation" and helps students assume **responsibility** for their own behavior, a hallmark of Invitational Learning.

The Programs

While Invitational Learning is much more than a program (Invitational Learning is the Christmas Tree, programs are the ornaments), programs have a significant influence on the ways people are treated. Like the places and policies mentioned earlier, programs can be helpful or harmful to individuals and groups.

One reason some programs are less than inviting is that they focus on narrow goals and neglect the wide scope of human concerns. For example, imagine a counseling center program that groups certain individuals together, gives them a label, and treats them all alike. The label itself becomes a stigma which negates the positive purposes for which the program was originally created. Similar things happen in schools, where tracking programs label students. People are not labels, and programs that label individuals as different can have negative effects.

An illustration of a program that can have long-lasting negative consequences is the "cutting" of an athletic squad. This painful business begins in the early years when boys and girls who would most benefit from athletic activity are informed that they did not make the squad. It is sad that while the great majority of elementary school children participate in organized athletics, the number dwindles to less than half that number in high school. A program that involves the rejection of many hopeful athletes by highly significant authority figures can have long-term negative consequences.

From an Invitational Learning viewpoint, the school that wins state championships while it discourages many young people from athletics has failed its responsibility. The school district that brags of its above average standardized test scores while accepting a high dropout rate has failed its responsibility. The counseling program that has a successful treatment rate but is based on coercion, fear, and lack of collaborative effort between provider and recipient has

The counseling program that has a successful treatment rate but is based on coercion, fear, and lack of collaborative effort between provider and recipient has failed its responsibility.

failed its responsibility. Once again the ends do not and never will justify the means.

An outstanding example of a program that is centered on the assumptions of Invitational Learning can be found at East Davidson High School in North Carolina. The entire faculty and staff of East Davidson made a commitment to reduce the dropout rate. Thanks to various incentive program activities, such as peer counseling, faculty mentoring, friendly competitions for attendance, and much hoopla, the dropout rate was reduced by 43 percent in one year. Invitational Learning requires that professional helpers closely monitor programs that add to, or detract from, its basic assumptions.

Advocates of Invitational Learning also stay informed about programs in the larger community. There are countless community programs that can contribute significantly to the goals of Invitational Learning. Programs range from free dental checkups, eyeglasses, and hearing aids to Big Brother, Hospice, and Alcoholics Anonymous. Every community program, regardless of how small or large, has the potential to contribute to the success of Invitational Learning.

Every community program, regardless of how small or large, has the potential to contribute to the success of Invitational Learning

The Processes

The fourth powerful "P" in Invitational Learning is embedded in the places, policies and programs discussed earlier. But process is so important that it deserves recognition in its own right.

There are countless ways in which process reveals itself. Little (1982) reported that educators in successful schools valued process. They participated in collegiality and professional development. They worked with each other to improve themselves and their school, and there was much conversation regarding instruction and preparation of materials.

Process represents not only the **content** of what is offered, but also the **context**. It represents not simply the **lyrics**, but the **melody**. The context and melody of Invitational Learning is that life is never so hurried that we have no time for a caring, civil, polite, and courteous stance. Any learning that takes place under conditions of high stress, such as lack of concern, rudeness, or insults, is likely to disappear when the sources of the stress are removed.

The reason process is so important in Invitational Learning is that it reminds us that **how** we teach or counsel and **how** we act while we're doing these things are far more important in the long run than **what** students or clients learn. A beautiful example of this process was provided by a former student:

> I remember the time that I was at my desk, and I was twisting a ring around my finger. My teacher must have noticed, because he said, "Paula, I can tell that you're nervous about something. May I help?" Well, I was so impressed because I thought he could read my mind. I also thought what a marvelous person to be so perceptive and to really take the time to know and care how I felt inside.

The inviting behavior of a single professional helper may not be sufficient, but it is always significant. Frequently, it is the power of one genuine, caring helping behavior that encourages clients toward a more responsible and beneficial lifestyle. Thus, a single inviting act becomes the catalyst for success.

The People

We saved **people**, the fifth "P," for last because people are the most important part of Invitational Learning and the most challenging. Places, policies, programs, and processes are vital, but it is the people that create and maintain Invitational Learning. In most helping relationships, recipients seek assistance through the interactions they have with people in their lives. A sound knowledge of human development, including developmental stages, social and psychological processes, and the principles of learning and behavior, is essential for helping professionals who wish to employ Invitational Learning. This knowledge is not only applied to achieve understanding of client or student development, but also to gain an appreciation of how other significant people in the client's life are contributing to or detracting from his or her existence and development. Specifically, Invitational Learning enables the helper to

Frequently, it is the power of one genuine, caring helping behavior that encourages clients toward a more responsible and beneficial lifestyle.

...it is the people that create and maintain Invitational Learning.

evaluate the personal and professional levels of functioning encountered by the client in daily interactions.

Assessment of people's dominant level of functioning allows the counselor or other helper to make appropriate decisions about the strategies or approaches that may be beneficial in the helping process. For example, an employee assistance counselor, who assesses that a worker's poor job performance is related to dissatisfaction and dysfunction in the family, may choose to invite the spouse and children in for counseling together. In this manner, the counselor views all the people in the worker's family as vital pieces to the puzzle of how to improve job performance and career satisfaction.

A further example of the primacy of people in Invitational Learning was provided by a high school counselor:

> There are those students who act like they don't want to be invited. They come to school with their heads shaved and wearing black leather jackets. They sit in the back of the classroom with their chairs raised back. They seem to be saying that nobody likes them and they don't like "nobody neither." I worked with one such student for a number of counseling sessions with little success, but I was determined not to give up. I knew that I was the last hold the school had on this boy. At the conclusion of one counseling session, I asked the boy if he knew where I might buy some wood for my home fireplace (I was new in town). He was vague in his response. At my home the next evening I happened to look out the window and there was a beautiful stack of firewood in my back yard. To this day I wonder (with some apprehension) where the boy and his friends got that firewood! But, that firewood was the beginning of a successful counseling relationship.

Those of us who use Invitational Learning understand that it is important to let our clients and students know that we will not give up on them. We give what we have and expect positive results.

Unfortunately, it sometimes happens that decisions which have long-lasting impact on people's lives are made for reasons of effectiveness, efficiency, and conformity that have little or no relationship to the welfare of the people involved. Invitational Learning is based on the proper regard for the value of **places, policies, programs,** and **processes,** but **people** come first. It strongly urges altering, to the extent possible, those forces that directly or indirectly inconvenience people or inhibit their development. As an integrative approach to professional helping, Invitational Learning is based on the recognition that successful assistance is more likely when helpers and their students and clients consider all the factors that influence human existence and potential. In particular, the five powerful "P's": **places, policies, programs, processes,** and **people** are viewed as a whole greater than the sum of its parts. Using the five "P's" as a guide, teachers, social workers, counselors, nurses and other professional helpers can create an optimally inviting **total** environment for themselves and for those with whom they work. Chapter 5 will present The Four Corner Press and demonstrate how the helper's self-as-instrument can be strengthened and enhanced.

Chapter 5

The Four Corner Press

*Personal growth must precede professional growth.
What you do in your profession is a function of the
person you are. That must, therefore, be your top
priority.*

This Running Life
—George Sheehan

This concluding chapter of Part I seeks to tie everything together. In addition to: (1) identifying the core values of **respect, trust, optimism,** and **intentionality,** (2) presenting the perceptual tradition and the importance of self-concept theory, (3) introducing the five powerful "P's" and (4) describing the four levels of functioning, Invitational Learning also offers a blueprint for action which we call the "Four Corner Press." Each corner represents a vital dimension of successful living. The Four Corners are:

*Invitational
Learning also
offers a blueprint
for action which
we call the "Four
Corner Press."*

1. Being Personally Inviting With Oneself.	2. Being Personally Inviting With Others.
3. Being Professionally Inviting With Oneself.	4. Being Professionally Inviting With Others.

Professionals who accept Invitational Learning understand that consistent relationships can best be achieved when we use helping behaviors in all our endeavors. This follows the ancient Greek ideal of balance among our emotional, spiritual, intellectual, and physical selves. Invitational Learning requires that helpers orchestrate their lives in each of the four corners to avoid disharmony and fragmentation. The goal is to "tune" our lives so that each of the four corners is in concert with all others. Like pistons in a finely-tuned automobile, the four work together to give power to the whole movement. While there are times when one of the four corners will demand special attention, the overall goal is synchronization. It would be improbable that counselors and others could maintain a high level of functioning in one area of their lives while functioning at a disinviting level in another area.

It is possible that we could devote so much energy to certain relationships in our life, that others might be neglected. Invitational Learning recognizes this risk and encourages helpers to try and focus proportionately on four areas of their lives. Each area is important in becoming and being a successful professional helper because each contributes to a balance between personal and professional development.

Being Personally Inviting With Oneself

In case of the loss of cabin pressure, you first place the mask over your own face and then place the mask on the face of your children.

—Airline Flight Attendant

To achieve the highest level of human interaction and to be a beneficial presence in the lives of others, we should first be inviting with ourselves.

As simple as it sounds, being personally inviting with ourselves is not easy. From childhood, most of us have been taught the evils of "selfishness," "pride," "egotism," "self-centeredness," and "conceit." Yet trust in and respect for oneself as well as optimism and intentionality are required to be inviting with oneself emotionally, intellectually, and physically. Caring for ourselves places us in the best position to help others.

To achieve the highest level of human interaction and to be a beneficial presence in the lives of others, we should first be inviting with ourselves. To rephrase the axiom: "Invitations begin at home." This means sending messages to ourselves that recognize our value, worth, and responsibility.

Invitations to ourselves take a variety of forms and a spectrum of important areas. For example, by eating well, exercising regularly, participating in sports or other recreational activities we take care of our physical selves. This is an important personal invitation for professional helpers to send ourselves because helping is demanding. If we as professional helpers are not physically fit and do not have the stamina to survive the challenges of our jobs, it is unlikely we will be able to maintain an optimistic, inviting posture. What follows are some practical ways to care for ourselves emotionally, intellectually, and physically.

Being personally inviting with oneself requires attention to one's feelings, practicing positive and realistic self-talk, and learning relaxation techniques. It means caring for one's mental health and learning to make appropriate choices in life. By taking up a new hobby, relaxing with a good novel, spending time alone, or experiencing spiritual renewal, a person can rejuvenate his or her emotional well-being. Here are sample ways of being personally inviting with oneself emotionally.

Get sufficient sleep	Monitor your internal dialogue
Develop loving relationships	Get there early
Buy something new	Grow a garden
Take a bubble bath	Try a new recipe
Allow for private time	Have lunch with a friend
Learn to laugh more	Get tickets to a play
Try a new cereal	Rearrange the furniture
Attack your clothes closet	Value your uniqueness
Compliment yourself	Listen to good music
Celebrate holidays	

Being inviting with ourselves intellectually means to keep our blade bright, not to "rust" on our laurels.

Ways to invite ourselves emotionally are limited only by our imagination.

Being inviting with ourselves intellectually means to keep our blade bright, not to "rust" on our laurels. For any human to develop optimally requires intellectual stimulation. A basic rule for achieving a long life is don't become **stiff, fat,** or **bored.** Living an intellectual life means to participate in a wide variety of activities that increase knowledge, sharpen thought processes, and improve the

A basic rule for achieving a long life is don't become stiff, fat, or bored.

overall powers of the mind. Joining discussion groups, nature clubs, science societies and art centers are only a few of the countless ways we can be personally inviting with ourselves intellectually. Here are more samples:

Write a paper	Participate in politics
Browse through a library	Start a collection
Work on a degree	Take a course
Visit a museum	Join a book club
Share a hobby	Learn a new sport
Keep up with current events	Subscribe to magazines
Maintain a learning posture	Commit to a great cause
Watch quality television	

Professionals who expand their intellectual horizons recognize the subtle but significant connections among emotional, intellectual, spiritual, and physical health.

When our physical selves are neglected or in disrepair, it is unlikely that we can maintain emotional health or expand ourselves intellectually. Invitational Learning requires a commitment to care for the physical self. Most people are not too concerned about their physical health until they are at risk of losing it. From an Invitational Learning stance, each individual has the moral obligation to take care of one's physical self.

While a comprehensive list of ways to care for ourselves physically is virtually limitless here are samples:

Get medical care when needed	Take long walks
Avoid high cholesterol foods	Eliminate smoking
Develop positive food habits	Drink lots of water
Fasten your safety belt	Maintain dental hygiene
Join a gym class	Get a massage
Take stairs instead of elevator	Beware of junk food
Maintain one clothing size	Exercise at home
Ration intake of salt	Go to a spa
Breath fresh air	Practice defensive driving
Visit the dentist on schedule	Arrange an annual physical checkup

For the apathetic person, existence itself can be a burden; for the enthusiastic, good health is a marvelous possibility for being and becoming.

There are countless ways to be personally inviting with ourselves that go beyond the emotional, intellectual, and physical suggestions mentioned here. But while being personally inviting with oneself is necessary, it is not sufficient. People are social beings who require the company of others. This being so, Invitational Learning stresses the value of being personally inviting with others.

Being Personally Inviting With Others

To forget a friend is sad — not everyone has had a friend.
The Little Prince
—Antoine De Saint-Exupery

Invitational Learning requires that the feelings, wishes, and aspirations of other people be taken into account. Without this, Invitational Learning would not exist. Relationships are like gardens, they require cultivation and nourishment if they are to survive and flourish. Our own well-being is dependent on the well-being of those we love and who love us in return. To realize our relatively boundless potential we depend on the continuing nurturing of fellow human beings.

Invitational Learning requires that the feelings, wishes, and aspirations of other people be taken into account.

While it is wise to take time to be alone, it should not be too often or too long. Helping professionals understand the importance of sending and receiving positive messages to and from family, friends and colleagues. (From an Invitational Learning viewpoint, the "social committee" is probably the most important committee in any organization). Without this social affirmation, we are unlikely to develop at all, except as shriveled fragments of what could have been. Here are sample ways of being personally inviting with others:

Get to know neighbors	Form a carpool
Send friendly notes	Remember birthdays
Take time to listen	Telephone a friend
Invite someone to lunch	Have a dinner party
Use good manners	Smile often
Join a celebration	Enjoy hoopla
Do something nice	Contact an old friend
Establish rituals	Wire some flowers
Visit relatives	Join a team
Attend a religious observance	

Once the desire (Invitational Learning) is in place, the behavioral opportunities are countless. For example, a high school counselor was reviewing the progress in a helping relationship when he asked the student: "What is the most significant thing that has happened since we began working together?" The client replied: "When you made me a cup of hot tea." An invitation to feel able, valuable and responsible can be a very small thing, but each invitation has boundless potential.

An invitation to feel able, valuable and responsible can be a very small thing, but each invitation has boundless potential.

Positive experiences in our personal relationships with others contribute significantly to our own personal development and simultaneously enhance our capability of forming beneficial professional relationships. By being personally inviting with ourselves and others, we facilitate and optimize our potential to become professionally inviting with ourselves and others, as well.

Being Professionally Inviting With Oneself

"I can't believe that," said Alice. "Can't you?" the Queen said in a pitying tone. "Try again: draw a long breath and shut your eyes." Alice laughed. "There's no use trying," she said: "One can't believe impossible things." "I daresay you haven't had much practice," said the Queen. "When I was your age, I always did it for half an hour a day. Why, sometimes I've believed as many as six impossible things before breakfast."

Alice in Wonderland
—Lewis Carroll

It is important to keep our imaginations intact, our thirst for knowledge unquenched, and to travel new roads...

As the Queen pointed out, it is important for us to imagine impossible things. It is important to keep our imaginations intact, our thirst for knowledge unquenched, and to travel new roads if we are to ensure our continuing development. Professionals, including counselors, teachers, nurses, and allied human service personnel, spend years in academic training to acquire their skills. These years of formal study conclude with degrees, certificates, diplomas, and licenses. However, those who accept Invitational Learning continue their development. By updating skills, mastering new techniques, thinking new thoughts, learning new research findings, and locating fresh ways to rekindle the fires of professionalism.

Being professionally inviting with oneself can take a variety of forms. Professionals who return to graduate school, enroll in a weekend workshop, attend conferences, read journals, write for publication, or conduct their own research, are keeping themselves young professionally. They avoid stagnation and the danger of becoming outmoded in their knowledge and approaches to human service.

Keeping alive professionally is particularly important in the helping professions because of the rapidly expanding knowledge base regarding humans and their development. Perhaps never before have knowledge, techniques, and innovations been so bountiful. Counselors, teachers, and other professionals must paddle their canoes harder than ever just to stay abreast of developments. Here are some practical suggestions of ways to keep up to date:

Try a new method	Dress professionally
Seek certification	Join professional groups
Write a professional article	Attend a conference
Learn a new skill	Brighten your office
Welcome change	Be ethically aware
Release your imagination	Manage your time
Write down your thoughts	Serve on Boards
Read professional journals	Arrive early
Encourage professional exchanges	

One of our graduate students captured the concept of being professionally inviting with oneself when she wrote: " I am the best 'me' there is, I am a V.I.P.—Very Invited Person." We now turn our attention to the final corner of the Four Corner Press: Being Professionally Inviting with Others.

Being Professionally Inviting With Others

The meaning of life lies in the chance it gives us to produce, or to contribute to, something greater than ourselves.

On The Meaning of Life
—Will Durant

Success in being personally inviting with oneself and others, and being professionally inviting with oneself, leads counselors and other helpers to the fourth and most important area to their clients, to be professionally inviting with others. Invitational Learning addresses two skill areas that contribute to our ability to be professionally inviting with others: communication and evaluation.

Helpers who seek a high level of communication skills, who wish to realize the "Plus Factor" mentioned in Chapter 3, work hard on their listening skills: their ability to hear, to accept, and to reflect their clients' feelings. When these basic skills are in place, the helper is on sound footing to establish healthy and productive professional relationships.

When these skills are complemented by specific methods of evaluating outcomes to assure appropriate direction, we validate ourselves as professionals. Being professionally inviting with others implies a consistent process of responsibility for the helping behaviors we choose. This responsibility enables us to evaluate the approaches and strategies we have selected and to modify them where appropriate.

Many approaches used by counselors, teachers, and allied helpers are compatible. As noted earlier, Invitational Learning incorporates many policies, programs, and processes. In fact, Invitational Learning strongly encourages professional helpers to integrate varying approaches and techniques into a consistent and reliable practice so long as they are consistent with its basic assumptions.

Here is a "sampler" of the countless ways professional helpers can be professionally inviting with others:

Share your talents	Offer professional feedback
Form support groups	Network with colleagues
Be a mentor	Make signs inviting
Be available for speaking	Help younger colleagues
Work cooperatively	Maintain an optimistic stance
Share decision making	Evaluate the Five "P's" often
Work to remember names	Be honest & trustworthy
Avoid paralysis of analysis	Treat people as individuals
Roll with the punches	Fight racism in any form
Be aware of and avoid sexist language	Recognize accomplishments of others

The professionally inviting behaviors we share with others largely determine what others share with us. And is there anyone who wants to be disinvited by his or her associates rather than invited?

The Four Corner Press of Invitational Learning is to be (1) personally inviting with oneself, (2) personally inviting with others, (3) professionally inviting with oneself, and (4) professionally inviting with others. The Four Corner Press offers valuable guidelines for personal and professional functioning. Professional helpers who are able to balance and orchestrate these four corners into a seamless whole are on the way to mastering Invitational Learning.

In the first part of this monograph we have explored the major facets of Invitational Learning. By focusing on its basic assumptions, its theoretical foundations, the four levels of functioning, the "five powerful P's," and the Four Corner Press, we have highlighted familiar but often overlooked forces that contribute so significantly to success or failure in human existence and development.

Now it is up to you, the professional helper. If Invitational Learning is to be an integral part of your personal and professional life, it will be because of your trust, respect, optimism and intentionality. And the beautiful compensation of inviting others to realize their potential is that you will be inviting the realization of your own potential as well. Part II of this monograph presents the practice of Invitational Learning by experts in the field.

The professionally inviting behaviors we share with others largely determine what others share with us.

Part II

The Practice: Voices From the Field

Our greatest duty and our main responsibility is to help others. But please, if you can't help them, would you please not hurt them.

—The Dalai Lama of Tibet

Chapter 6

The Baltimore County Guidance and Counseling Experience

Donald E. McBrien

What Attracted You to the Invitational Model?

How do you invite 240 professional school counselors both personally and professionally to develop effective comprehensive programs, and in turn invite 80,000 students to achieve their fullest potential? In essence this question brought Baltimore County Public Schools, particularly the guidance and counseling program, to the invitational paradigm developed by Purkey, Novak, Schmidt and others (Purkey & Novak, 1984; Purkey & Schmidt, 1987).

The individual student about whom we have several fundamental beliefs is at the center of our guidance and counseling program. First, we believe that each student has the potential for growth and that, by nature, students are growth-oriented. Second, we believe human development is enhanced by one's belief in self, which is fostered by relationships imbued with realistic and genuine levels of optimism, trust, and respect. Third, we are in the process of continually sending positive and negative messages to others, and the view we hold about ourselves is the direct result of the impact these messages have on us. Fourth, the sense of control we have over our destiny is in direct relationship to the value we attribute to ourselves. Additionally, our sense of control is reflected in our willingness to plan, to be goal-directed and to invest in tomorrow. Fifth, the more value we attribute to ourselves the more willing we are to risk our minds and hearts with others, and thus the more

The individual student about whom we have several fundamental beliefs is at the center of our guidance and counseling program.

likely we are to develop into fully functioning, healthy human beings.

It is clear to us that what we believe as a school system is congruent with Invitational Learning. In particular, it strongly parallels the beliefs and goals of our school guidance and counseling program. Adoption of this paradigm places our program in a wholistic and systematic framework. This framework suggests that schools should educate the whole child and comprehensive school counseling programs should provide planned sequential services for all students. In addition, the four levels of invitational behavior are easily translated to all populations because they are defined in layperson's terms and use analogies and metaphors familiar to most people.

The concept of personal and professional invitations presents a meaningful way of viewing counselor functioning and development. The focal points for invitational interventions—people, places, programs, policies, and processes—encompass all aspects of the school guidance and counseling program. Finally, and perhaps most importantly, many school counselors believe self-concept theory to be useful as an orientation for understanding human behavior.

We are not sure if Baltimore County Public Schools found Invitational Learning or Invitational Learning found us.

We are not sure if Baltimore County Public Schools found Invitational Learning or Invitational Learning found us. Of this we are sure: It has provided a structure by which we can integrate guidance activities into the learning process and emphasize the continuing development of our pre-kindergarten through senior high school counseling program, which strives to serve all students, school staff members, and parents.

What Strategy Did You Use in Gaining Adoption of the Model?

A major change in the state's focus in school counseling programs precipitated the invitational approach to our school services. This new program emphasis required counselors to focus on student outcomes in relation to three state-wide goals: personal, social, and career development. Previously, guidance and counseling programs were either process directed (time was allotted to different processes such as one-to-one counseling, group counseling or consultation) or they were service directed (they focused on the delivery of specific services such as personal counseling, career guidance, and informational activities).

This outcome-oriented approach to program delivery created a need for counselors to conceptualize student outcomes in relation to school success, decision-making competencies, and interpersonal relationships. In our program, we agreed that student outcomes, regardless of the domain—personal, social, or career development—should be defined by movement toward autonomy appropriate to the developmental level of the student. We set goals to enable students to begin to think "I can" rather than "I can't" and to encourage them to adopt an optimistic attitude in their lives. In brief, we aimed to enable all students to become intentionally invited to the celebration of learning.

Dr. William Purkey was invited to speak on self-concept and school success to all of our school counselors. Everyone was immediately attracted to his ideas. Counselors saw in Invitational Learning an attitude towards human development that they already embraced. Subsequent staff development activities were offered, including a three-day workshop on the principles of the invitational model. What emerged from these staff development activities was an invitational orientation to guidance and counseling services, with student outcomes being defined from the perspective of the "invited student." In brief, each of our program goals was translated into invitational statements.

While most counselors quickly adopted the philosophy and assumptions of Invitational Learning, a few became frustrated because the invitational concepts were not presented in pragmatic "how to do" strategies. However, as these counselors began to grasp the freeing nature of using a variety of approaches to helping students rather than the old prescriptive and restrictive orientations to counseling, they were excited and willing to view their work within the invitational context.

Two aspects of Invitational Learning that were particularly well received, both from a personal and a professional perspective, were the four levels of functioning (intentionally inviting, unintentionally inviting, unintentionally disinviting and intentionally disinviting), and the identification of five areas of intervention (people, places,

We set goals to enable students to begin to think "I can" rather than "I can't" and to encourage them to adopt an optimistic attitude....

policies, programs, and processes). Both the invitational levels and the intervention points were easily translated into program objectives and subsequently into a model for program planning, delivery and evaluation. Thus, our invitational guidance and counseling program was born.

How Does Invitational Learning Function in Your Setting?

The inviting guidance and counseling program is a planned program of services directed to specific student outcomes and focused on individual and school needs. Our management plan articulates the counselors' program within specific time parameters. Included in the plan is a program evaluation process that assesses the plan's effectiveness in reducing student needs and concerns. The management plan defines the way in which counselors will use resources and processes to reduce student concerns.

All guidance and counseling plans are based on a needs assessment conducted annually in each school.

All guidance and counseling plans are based on a needs assessment conducted annually in each school. A large question bank has been developed by counselors that teases out data reflective of the three state and local guidance and counseling goals. (This question bank is available on request from Dr. Donald McBrien, Director of Pupil Services, Baltimore County Public Schools, Towson, MD 21204.) Data derived from the needs assessment becomes the basis for the management plan and for its subsequent evaluation.

Each guidance and counseling plan takes into account that assisting students with their concerns is influenced by one or more of the five key interventional points—people, places, programs, policies, and processes. If the needs assessment reveals, for example, that students do not feel invited in the areas of personal development, all five intervention points would be analyzed as possible contributing factors to this disinviting view. Specific strategies to reduce the negative effects of each intervention point would be identified as the result of this analysis. Additionally, those aspects of the counseling process that have positive impact on students would be strengthened. Since all guidance and counseling plans are directed to student outcomes, issues related to counselor "role function" or "turf protection" are minimized. Also, since the plan came from the local school staff and not the central office, "top down" management issues are avoided. Finally, program evaluation is the responsibility of the local school and is separated from counselor evaluation, which is assigned to the school principal.

Thus far, this school-based management approach has resulted in counselors feeling more in control of their programs. With this feeling of control also comes a feeling of responsibility and ownership. Counselors see more clearly the need to upgrade skills, and they become more involved in staff development that is provided at the school level. Staff development occurs because counselors have identified a need to receive it and thus they are more committed to it. In this way, counselors invite themselves professionally.

In addition to staff development, counselors also have been invited both professionally and personally to serve as mentors to other counselors. Each year we hire at least ten and sometimes as many as 30 new counselors. These new counselors are each assigned a mentor counselor. The mentoring approach to assisting new counselors has been well received by both the new personnel and their mentors. Mentoring, like inviting, is clearly a mutually beneficial experience.

A major thrust of the inviting guidance and counseling program is its emphasis on intentionality. If a program does not reflect intentionality, it becomes a set of random activities with no sense of purpose or direction: It becomes a program that lacks care and respect, refutes trust and reflects a shallowness of intent.

To foster a high level of intentionality, all the counselors were introduced to the concept of situational analysis. Situational analysis requires counselors to examine the condition of the individuals to be served within the context of the situations in which the individuals are involved (Hersey & Blanchard, 1982; Ivey, 1986).

The level of functioning or condition of a client is defined by his or her orientation to specific tasks, and by the person's psychological investment in the situation. Four levels of client functioning are defined: unwilling and unable, willing and unable, able and unwilling, willing and able. Each level of functioning involves the satisfaction of specific needs (Hersey & Blanchard, 1982). The unable and

...this school-based management approach has resulted in counselors feeling more in control of their programs.

unwilling have security needs, the unable and willing have security and social or relationship needs, the able and unwilling have social and esteem needs, and the willing and able students have self-actualization needs.

...when a counselor, teacher or other helper communicates with students at the appropriate need level, the student perceives the message as intentionally inviting.

It is hypothesized that when a counselor, teacher or other helper communicates with students at the appropriate need level, the student perceives the message as intentionally inviting. Thus, we develop an intentionally inviting program when interventions occur in each of the five areas—people, places, policies, programs, and processes—and when these interventions address the needs of students.

How Successful Has the Program Been to Date?

Criteria have been established to measure the success of the invitational guidance and counseling program. These criteria address both programmatic issues and counselor performance by examining a series of questions:

1. **Are guidance and counseling management plans being developed, implemented and updated on an annual basis, and do these plans address the unique needs of the individual school?** Since the adoption of the model, the answer is consistently, "Yes." All elementary and secondary schools and vocational technical centers have a plan that meets both criteria. Not only do the plans exist, they also have been approved by local school advisory committees and the school administration.

Principals frequently use data derived from the counselor's needs assessment in goal setting for their entire school. Also, program impact evaluations not only provide counselors with subsequent program direction, they also provide administrators with information about the condition of the student body. Impact evaluation data also have assisted the central office staff in designing staff development activities and in budgeting for specific resources and materials.

Probably no greater tribute to the quality of a program exists than the honor of being cited as a model program.

2. **Is the quality of services provided by counselors to students, staff and parents being adequately recognized?** Again our findings say, "Yes." Probably no greater tribute to the quality of a program exists than the honor of being cited as a model program. Central office guidance supervisors and

school counselors have presented their programs, demonstrated skills, and shared with school board members the invitational guidance and counseling program. One county that recently initiated an elementary school counseling program attributed their program's birth to Baltimore County's elementary guidance and counseling program.

All four county supervisors have been recognized by the state's school counselor association for their outstanding contribution to the profession. Recognition has come from numerous parents and parent-teacher organizations who took a strong stand with the county Board of Education and county fiscal authorities for additional counselor positions. Elementary school administrators responding to the super-intendent's request for staffing priorities listed additional guidance and counseling services as their number one priority, placing it above reduced class size. In Baltimore County, counselors are perceived as service providers, not as administrators or clerical personnel.

3. **Is there evidence that the school counselor feels invited both personally and professionally?** Again, the answer is "Yes." While it is difficult to speak to the level of personal satisfaction counselors experience, we can infer from their long tenure, willingness to extend their work beyond what the teacher contract requires, and the overall high level of camaraderie demonstrated at all counselor functions that counselors in our system do feel personally invited.

It is less difficult to measure the pulse of the counselors' professional commitment, which is highly visible in Baltimore County. More than 90 counselors are National Board Certified Counselors or are in the process of obtaining that certification. Over 70 percent of all counselors attend at least one national or state professional conference (on their own time and without county reimbursement) during any given school year. Most counselors have at least 30 hours of graduate work beyond their masters degree, four have earned doctorates and others are in the final stages of their doctoral studies. In a typical year, many counselors will make presentations at national and state conferences, and almost all counselors present to local PTA, church and civic organizations. Ten counselors and central staff members have been identified as outstanding educators by the

In Baltimore County, counselors are perceived as service providers, not as adminis-trators or clerical personnel.

county teacher organizations or by the Baltimore Chamber of Commerce. A member of the central office staff is a past-president of ASCA (American School Counselor Association) and AACD (American Association for Counseling and Development), and all members of the central office staff have served as president of state ACD chapters or divisions. Many counselors have held similar positions at the state and local levels. Clearly, our cadre of 240 counselors demonstrates professional commitment.

What Plans and Goals Do You Contemplate for the Future?

The current success of the program mandates that every effort be made to continue the student-centered invitational guidance and counseling programs. A major goal for the next five years is the orientation of new counselors to Invitational Learning. This will require ongoing staff development for new personnel and an increase in our mentoring program. Additionally, guidance department chairpersons, who are the school-based managers of this program, need to develop additional planning and evaluation skills.

...guidance department chairpersons, who are the school-based managers of this program, need to develop additional planning and evaluation skills.

Staff development for the future will refine the invitational approach within the framework of personal and social counseling, career development services, and interventions with special populations such as handicapped, gifted/talented, and at-risk students. Emphasis will be placed on counseling processes and consulting skills. Counselor interventions with parents and the development of parent education programs that parallel Invitational Learning are currently being developed by counselors at the elementary and secondary levels.

There are no plans for major revisions or deletions from the school counseling program, but broader input in the planning and evaluation phases is being considered. We expect that within a five-year period the recipients of our counseling services will have an increasing voice in the program's emphasis and development. One major addition to our guidance and counseling program will be the use of paraprofessionals and computer-assisted support. As these new human resources become available, it will be imperative that they adhere to the principles of Invitational Learning.

What Advice Would You Offer to New Implementers of This Model?

To implement Invitational Learning in a comprehensive guidance and counseling program, all school counselors must become conversant with the practical application of self-concept theory and perceptual psychology. A major pitfall can occur when counselors and other professional helpers, who do not understand self-concept theory and perceptual psychology, are asked to interpret and apply Invitational Learning. Too often, uninformed practitioners naively present a litany of "how to's" but then falter when they are asked to develop a sound rationale for their practices.

To be inviting personally and professionally one must genuinely exhibit trust, respect, and optimism in an intentional manner. Such intentionality is illustrated by a dependable, consistent and effective level of professional functioning. Effective counselors typically exhibit all these characteristics, yet experiences should be provided to assist counselors in continuously evaluating their behaviors and levels of functioning.

School administrators, central office staff and other professionals who supervise the school guidance and counseling program must also be committed to the invitational approach. Too frequently, programs with great potential go astray because significant numbers of program participants are not ready or willing to accept something new. It is imperative that everyone who will participate in an Invitational Learning program develop sufficient fluency with its content and become invested in it. Patience is a critical variable if Invitational Learning or any other educational model is to be accepted.

Too frequently, programs with great potential go astray because significant numbers of program participants are not ready or willing to accept something new.

Chapter 7

The Furman University Center for Excellence Experience

Judy Lehr

What Attracted You to the Invitational Learning Model?

I became acquainted with the concept of Invitational Learning during my first year of teaching. The year was 1972 and I had moved to South Carolina to get married and begin my career. The experiences I had those first few months are still crystal clear in my memory. I was energetic and enthusiastic, ready to shape the lives of young people.

My first assignment was as a resource teacher. The personnel director of the school system explained, "Judy, you will be working with a few students who need some extra help in reading and math." I set up my classroom just as my college professors had taught me, with chairs in straight rows and the teacher's desk in front. My lesson plans were letter perfect with objectives covering all levels of Bloom's Taxonomy. I anticipated my students sitting still, listening to my clear lectures and attending to my demonstrations. My short- and long-term goals were written on a chart taped to my desk. I could hardly sleep the night before my first **big** day. I was well prepared and eager to begin.

I was sent 20 incorrigible students for a two-hour block. My students hated school and everything school stood for, especially the idea of being in a special class. I tried every trick of the trade, but nothing worked. I was a miserable failure who hated school as much as my students. My time was spent breaking up fights, begging students to do their work, and worrying about how to get through another day.

One day when things were at their worst, I wrote a letter of resignation. Before submitting the letter, I had the

I was energetic and enthusiastic, ready to shape the lives of young people.

opportunity to meet William Purkey and become acquainted with his principles of Invitational Learning. I remember clearly this principle: "Before you can teach kids, you must first invite them to learn. Make learning relevant to your students." Dr. Purkey voiced the usual educational attitudes, but he took another step and presented a framework to make schools more inviting for young people, to do things **with** students rather than **to** students.

William Purkey's message encouraged me to read his little book, *Self-Concept and School Achievement* (Purkey, 1971), and I decided to tear up my letter of resignation. Soon I began making major changes in my classroom and teaching style. I was determined to aim for "higher levels" of functioning, for both myself and my students.

Instead of a resource room, my classroom became a prevocational center.

The results were phenomenal. Instead of a resource room, my classroom became a prevocational center. Businesses donated a time clock, adding machine, old motors, and a variety of learning materials. Students would race to class to clock-in first and begin their individual work plans. We ordered social security cards, figured minimum wages, and learned reading, writing and mathematics in ways that were relevant to students. My kids enjoyed class, and I began to love teaching.

Since that initial success with the concept of Invitational Learning, I have used the principles throughout my educational career: as a staff development coordinator in a K-12 system; as a graduate research assistant at the University of Wisconsin in Madison working with the Individually Guided Education Project; as an elementary school principal; and finally at the university level as Director of Furman University's Center of Excellence Project.

What Strategies Did You Use in Gaining Acceptance and Adoption of the Invititational Learning Model?

The Center of Excellence began in 1985 with a small grant from the South Carolina Commission on Higher Education. Initially, 212 outstanding teachers were identified and asked to complete an open-ended questionnaire describing the skills/competencies needed to teach at-risk, low-achieving students. The results from this survey paralleled the model of Invitational Learning.

The major objective of the center is to apply the invitational model in local schools to make schools the most inviting places for everyone, but especially those hard-to-reach students often labeled "at-risk." Eight "model" elementary schools in the Upstate Schools Consortium have been a part of the Center of Excellence. The Upstate Schools Consortium is a group of 14 public school districts who have joined with Furman University to plan collaborative educational improvement programs.

In most participating schools an overview of the Center of Excellence was presented to the school staff. Additionally, a video entitled, "The Power of Positive Invitations," was shared with staff members. The video by William Purkey and Betty Siegel outlining the people, places, policies, programs, and processes of an inviting school was utilized. A number of invitational books, newsletters, and materials were purchased for the professional library of each project school. After a period of awareness, teams from each school participated in developing individual school plans. Gradually the teams moved from awareness, to understanding, to application, to adoption of the Invitational Learning Model.

Gradually the teams moved from awareness, to understanding, to application, to adoption of the Invitational Learning Model.

How Does the Invitational Learning Model Function in Your Program or Agency?

The current focus of the project is the middle school level. The BellSouth Foundation awarded Furman University and the South Carolina Upstate Schools Consortium a $170,000 grant to help fund a two-year project. Currently 13 middle schools representing seven school districts are participating.

The *Inviting Schools Survey* (see Appendix A) has been administered to the staff of each school in the Center of Excellence. The resulting data have been shared with local "teams" from each school who are completing a detailed item analysis. This information is being used to plan a summer institute and a comprehensive staff development program for each school based on the Invitational Learning Model. Seminars for staff during the first year of the project have included topics such as:

- Inviting Strategies That Work with At-Risk Students
- Needs and Learning Styles of the Disconnected Learner
- Boosting Students' Self-Esteem
- Building Esprit de Corps Within the Staff
- Motivating the Middle Level Student
- Thinking Skills for all Students
- Counseling Skills for Teachers

The school counselor has assumed a major leadership role on the majority of school teams. Because counselors have specialized educational backgrounds and experiences, they have been invaluable as a resource to share ideas with fellow staff members. Another major responsibility assumed by the counselor is the identification of a target group of at-risk students at each participating school. The following six-point criteria is used:

1. Two years below grade level in either reading or math, or not meeting BSAP standard;
2. Prior school suspension;
3. Participation in free or reduced lunch program;
4. Chronic absenteeism in the previous school year (15 days, excused or unexcused);
5. Retention at any grade level;
6. Teacher recommendation.

Many schools have implemented "Adopt-a-Student" programs to invite the at-risk student to stay in school.

Specific intervention strategies ranging from the formation of peer support groups to training in conflict resolution and tutorial programs have been developed. Many schools have implemented "Adopt-a-Student" programs to invite the at-risk student to stay in school.

For example, in some project schools each staff member has chosen to counsel at least one identified at-risk student who needs a special one-on-one relationship with a caring adult. In addition to tutoring these students, teachers often visit students' homes, take them out to dinner or sporting events, and reward them with small tokens for improved attendance and academic performance. The focus is on providing the student with the gift of quality time. The overall thrust of the student component is to examine the people, places, policies, programs, and processes that sometimes "disconnect" these students from the school and to design effective strategies to "re-connect" them.

How Successful Has the Invitational Learning Model Been to Date?

Elementary schools that have been part of the center report improved staff and student morale with a concomitant improvement in student test scores. The most dramatic improvement occurred at the first model school, Gateway Elementary in Travelers Rest, South Carolina, which received the *Inviting Schools Award* from the Alliance for Invitational Education (see Appendix B).

In 1986, when students took the *California Test of Basic Skill* (CTBS) their results were not as good as the principal, Glenn Wright, would have liked. For example, among fourth graders, 9 percent performed above expectation and 26 percent below expectation in reading on the CTBS; in language, 16 percent were above and 11 percent below; and in math, 11 percent were above, 8 percent below. In the 1987 testing of these children, the results showed 27 percent scored above expectation in reading skills with only 2 percent below; in language, 38 percent were above, 1 percent below; and in math, 57 percent scored above and 1 percent below. All grades showed improvement in test scores, with the fourth and fifth grades making the largest gains (Lehr & Harris, 1988).

The research design for the middle schools project includes comparison of data on the academic and self-concept measures of at-risk students. Discipline and attendance records are being monitored for changes. The *Inviting Schools Survey* is being used for pre- and post-test comparisons. These data will be available by the summer of 1990.

To prepare students for standardized testing, all students, especially those at risk, have been encouraged to do their best in a variety of innovative ways. Posters, a Rap Contest, and dress-up days using the school colors of red, white and blue (red for "use your head," white for "answer questions right," and blue for "to yourself be true") were successful in one middle school.

Teachers who monitor during the testing, distributed tickets to students who were "on task." These tickets could be used for a variety of rewards including a school dance, visit to the canteen, or five minutes of free time at lunch. Pep rallies were held to get students motivated about the tests. Student skills programs and extra tutorial services were provided to prepare students. One school-wide program that was particularly successful was the "WOW WORDS." Because CTBS and BSAP scores indicated that vocabulary was weak among students, a plan was devised to implement WOW.

In the WOW program, each day all students would meet new words selected from the South Carolina Word List for sixth through eighth grades. These words were announced on the intercom, posted throughout the school, and used by teachers in each subject area. Students would keep a notebook of the words and be quizzed each week. Test scores improved dramatically.

All schools are using the *CoRT Thinking Skills Program* (de Bono, 1986), which provides students with tools for problem solving. This process has been highly motivating to most students and many of those who are at risk seem to be changing their self-perception from "I am dumb" to "I am a thinker."

Each school has designed special programs to improve the self-esteem of the at-risk learner.

Each school has designed special programs to improve the self-esteem of the at-risk learner. Incentive programs have been implemented to reward students for improvement and effort. A conscious effort has been made to ensure that at-risk students are not left out when it comes to Honor Programs, Citizen of the Week, or other school-wide recognition programs.

In a recent project evaluation, teachers were asked to respond to the statement: "The most useful thing I have learned from the first year of this project is." Their comments follow and are illuminating:

➤ "The importance of being accepting in meeting the needs of disconnected students."
➤ "The importance of motivation and learning."
➤ "How to be a more inviting teacher."
➤ "Developing specific strategies to increase self-esteem in students."
➤ "All students can think at all levels. I encourage all students to higher levels of cognitive thinking."
➤ "The importance of getting to know my students better. For example, I use my lunch period to visit with my students."

➤ "Patience, the importance of high expectations, and general awareness of the needs of at-risk students."

Teachers also responded to this statement: "The impact of this project on our school has been:" Their comments included:

➤ "Improved attendance of at-risk learners."
➤ "Staff morale has increased."
➤ "Grades of targeted at-risk students are better."
➤ "Improvement in the self-image of the at-risk student."
➤ "Teachers are consciously trying to encourage and motivate at-risk students."
➤ "All students are getting more positive reinforcement."
➤ "At-risk students have a greater sense they belong to our school."
➤ "Teachers are now more aware of student problems."
➤ "Attitude and performance of students has improved."
➤ "Both students and teachers have benefited."
➤ "Our total school is a better place to be."

What Plans and Goals Do You Contemplate for the Future?

As a liberal arts university seeking to prepare the best possible teachers, we are aware of the necessity of having model schools to exemplify the practical application of current research on teaching and learning. We are committed to the Center of Excellence Project and to its goal of making schools the "most inviting places in town" for all students, but especially for those who are considered "at risk." The importance of a pre-service teacher's field experience—from the first observation to the culminating experience of student teaching—is absolutely vital. We are committed to our role of assisting educators in creating "model" schools. We plan to expand the middle school program to other school districts with the invitational model serving as the foundation for educational improvement.

...we are aware of the necessity of having model schools to exemplify the practical application of current research on teaching and learning.

What Advice Would You Offer to New Implementers of Invitational Learning?

Invitational Learning provides a framework for educational improvement. When implementing the model, first work to involve everyone in the process. Next, administer the *Inviting Schools Inventory* to the staff, selected students and parents. Form a team to plan specific strategies for school improvement based on the people, places, policies, programs, and processes of an inviting school. The composition of the team could include an administrator, teachers, counselors, parents, students, and perhaps a representative from a university, college, or the school system. Submit the plan developed by the school team, including objectives, activities, and the time line for completion to the total staff for approval before implementation. This site-based model of educational improvement will work and have lasting benefits. A caveat, of course, is do not attempt to change too quickly; target one objective at a time, and seek to do things with people, not to them.

...target one objective at a time, and seek to do things with people, not to them.

As a classroom teacher, staff development coordinator, school principal, and currently university professor, I am committed to the concept of Invitational Learning from first-hand experience. The future for education is promising as more and more schools implement the Invitational Learning Model.

Chapter 8

The East Davidson High School Experience

Debbie Chance

What Attracted You to the Invitational Learning Model?

Life as a first-year administrator was taking its toll as I walked through the double doors of the Sheraton Hotel in downtown Greensboro, North Carolina. I had decided to attend an Alliance for Invitational Education seminar at the end of the school year. I was dead tired, burned out, and scalded by a sense of frustration. I was questioning my ability as an administrator to challenge, motivate, and encourage.

The dropout rate at my high school was extraordinarily high and teacher morale was proportionately low. Torn between fight or flight, and seeking answers to my conundrum, I retreated into the conference room. On entering the room, I felt that I was among a very special group of educators and helping professionals. I was immediately attracted to their positivism and sense of purpose. I wanted to capture their philosophy, bottle it, and take it back to my school.

Our high school was soon to begin its ten-year accreditation for the Southern Association of Secondary Schools and Colleges (SACS). For 25 years we had stored our generic philosophy in the dusty, abandoned pages of previous accreditation reports. School philosophies are expected to be the foundation upon which all educational programs are based. Ours was on shaky ground. We needed a philosophical breath of life, a renaissance, a reason to be.

The Invitational Learning model, presented at the conference, encouraged teamwork, action, planning, and

I was questioning my ability as an administrator to challenge, motivate, and encourage.

We needed a philosophical breath of life, a renaissance, a reason to be.

71

goal-setting. The possibility of captivating our faculty with a very special cooperative approach led me to investigate the invitational view further.

The key to the effectiveness of Invitational Learning is teamwork. Faculty and staff need to feel a sense of ownership in their school philosophy. In comparison to the action-oriented stance of Invitational Learning, our school philosophy seemed commonplace and trivial, with meaningless phrases such as "to encourage the social, educational and psychological development of the student." I believed that Invitational Learning could give our school a rebirth.

In August of 1987, after attending the Alliance Conference, our high school invited William Purkey to deliver a kick-off address to the faculty, custodians, cafeteria staff, and parents at East Davidson High School in Thomasville, North Carolina. From this presentation many teachers asked to learn more about the invitational approach. An in-service program for renewal credit was developed so that these faculty members could read *Inviting School Success* (Purkey & Novak, 1984), and discuss its theories concerning self-concept and its relationship to students' academic and social success.

We introduced Invitational Learning as a possibility, not a necessity, as an opportunity, not a requirement.

We introduced Invitational Learning as a possibility, not a necessity, as an opportunity, not a requirement. The first priority was to establish a new school philosophy. A committee of teachers was formed with representation from the areas of English, social studies, science, and special education. A selection of parents and students also was invited to participate. The committee members assessed the old philosophy, analyzed its value, and made the recommendation to the faculty that it be revised to include the basic principles of Invitational Learning.

Because our faculty had been exposed to the concepts of invitational education, many teachers and staff readily embraced the "human potential" emphasis of Invitational Learning. We provided faculty with questionnaires addressing the possible adoption of these new invitational concepts, and we encouraged their honesty. Questions were as follows:

1. Are you satisfied with our current school philosophy?
2. Do you feel that we need to change our philosophy? If so, in what ways?

3. Please share your thoughts and feelings concerning the Invitational Learning Model?

The philosophy committee assessed the responses, and provided verbal and written reports of its findings. Based on these findings, the committee recommended that we draft a new philosophy based on a majority decision to move in this direction.

How Does Invitational Learning Function in Your School?

We emphasize teamwork. Committees in all disciplines of school life assess our programs, policies, and procedures. We teach the concepts of Invitational Learning to our students through example. Friendliness, courtesy, civility, and simple behaviors such as standing at doorways and welcoming students to class have been found to be powerful complements to our new, emerging philosophy.

We teach the concepts of Invitational Learning to our students through example.

During the first year of implementation, we held an Invitational Assembly in the school gymnasium, and the story of "I Am Lovable and Capable" was enacted using blue cards and orange cards (According to William Purkey's metaphor, orange cards represent intimidations, insults, and "disinvitations," while blue cards symbolize acceptance, positive regard, and "invitations.") With a DOA (Deadly Orange Attitude), our stage hero ended his day after multiple put-downs.

Our student council president delivered a dynamic speech on the importance of a positive attitude and a healthy self-concept, as well as the importance of realizing one's full potential. The school chorus ended the program with a song of "blue card sunshine" and inspiration.

As we returned to class, our new philosophy was alive and breathing in the hallways. Blue cards were signed and passed around all day. Positivism was racing through the bloodstream of our school. We enjoyed blue-iced cupcakes during the lunch period and our cafeteria team smiled and giggled as they gave them to students and staff.

Further efforts were made during our first "invitational year" to spruce up our school, both physically and psychologically. Here are a few examples of this year's activities:

...efforts were made during our first "invitational year" to spruce up our school, both physically and psychologically.

- The cafeteria was selected as our "invitational hub." Plants were hung from the ceiling and a student painted a fabulous mural covering an entire wall of the cafeteria. Furniture was donated by a local industry to spruce up the environment. And we brought in a salad bar and hot potato bar.
- Bulletin boards around the school boasted the "Power of Winning Notions" to encourage positive attitudes.
- Teachers dressed up their classrooms with comfortable chairs, couches, plants, and reading nooks.
- Trees, plants and flowers were planted to improve the school grounds.
- "Blue card" attitudes were present in every classroom.

For our second year, we began by teaching all students our philosophy and house rules. We organized an incentive committee made up of teachers and staff to brainstorm ways to infuse our curriculum with Invitational Learning and to reduce our dropout rate simultaneously.

The incentive committee was the steam engine that became the powerhouse behind many new programs. Some of these in the area of dropout prevention are:

1. **Teacher/Buddy System**. In this program each and every teacher in our school adopted a student who was at risk of dropping out. These students had a history of high absenteeism, academic failure and behavior problems. Teachers called when their students were absent from school and provided support and encouragement in many ways. They showed their adopted students that they cared, and helped these young students feel connected to our school family.

2. **Business Involvement**. Local businesses were encouraged to get involved by donating tee shirts, walkmans, tapes, meal vouchers, and other articles. Students were put on contracts by their teachers to raise their grades, increase attendance, and improve attitudes. When students met their goals, they won an incentive reward.

3. **Peer Helper Program**. The Peer Helper Program was another key component in our dropout prevention effort. Twenty-five students were trained in helping and leadership skills. The result of students supporting students

The result of students supporting students has been monumental. We encourage "drop-ins" not dropouts.

has been monumental. We encourage "drops-ins" not dropouts.

4. **Attendance Contests**. Attendance contests between classes were begun. The classes with the highest attendance percentage win a pizza party. We have a phrase at the high school that says: "East Davidson is a place where just being here makes a big difference." And it does!

5. **SMART**. We established a SMART committee (Student Management At-Risk Team). Composed of teachers, counselors, a social worker, and an administrator, this committee holds regular meetings to review case studies of students who are high risk for school failure and dropping out. The committee assists with interventions and collaboratively seeks ways to keep these students connected to school and the learning process.

The success of our inviting school is attributed to the fact that almost everyone jumped on the band wagon, and no one got off! Teamwork was essential. The invitational approach encourages the cooperative effort of all personnel and identifies all people as able, valuable and responsible. Our staff and students verified these philosophical tenants through their personal interactions as well as their commitment to our school's philosophy.

The success of our inviting school is attributed to the fact that almost everyone jumped on the band wagon, and no one got off!

How Successful Has Invitational Learning Been in Your School?

The highlight of our success occurred when the Governor of North Carolina, Jim Martin, arrived by helicopter on the front lawn of East Davidson High School on May 17, 1989. Our incentive committee had made sure that our school would get a giant "blue card" by securing the Governor's attention for our Invitational Celebration. Our dropout rate had been cut by 44 percent as a result of our inviting school programs, and we were ready to toot our horn!

For this "blue sunshine day," we invited our business partners, PTA, parents, athletic and band boosters, and community leaders to join us in our celebration. During the assembly, Dr. Purkey and Governor Martin validated and praised our invitational programs. We provided an overview of all our inviting school programs and recognized the efforts of our teachers, parents, students, and community

Our dropout rate had been cut by 44 percent as a result of our inviting school programs, and we were ready to toot our horn!

leaders. Governor Martin mentioned that he was keenly interested in lowering the dropout rate, and had set a goal of cutting it in half by the year 2000. "But you, here at East, about cut it in half in just one year," he said. "You took the philosophy of Invitational Learning and made it work with team effort."

Our day in the blue sunshine culminated with the gubernatorial helicopter lifting off the ground. Our hearts and spirits flew up into the atmosphere as we stood on the school lawn and watched the helicopter disappear into the horizon. We had experienced a very good year.

What Plans and Goals Do You Have for the Future?

Next year we plan to follow up with further efforts to cut our dropout rate and continue creating an inviting school environment. Our plans include:

We are going after "big business" partners for next year's programs.

1. Presenting a dropout prevention program complete with objectives and strategies for implementation to a major grocery chain. We are going after "big business" partners for next year's programs.
2. Providing more collaboration with teachers working together on SMART teams. By using a faculty-wide team approach, we can divide the "high-risk" student load more evenly and provide more quality time for each student.
3. Identifying ninth graders who have attendance problems, low academic performance, and behavior concerns early in the school year. After identifying these students, we plan to replace their "elective class" with a life-skills class, which will focus on self-concept development, study skills, work habits, healthy attitudes, and personalized tutoring.
4. Working on a "Business Buddy" program in which an area business person adopts a potential dropout and works with the student on a personal basis. Training for this program will be provided this summer by a local counseling agency.
5. Planning staff development to hone in on dropout prevention and the further development of our inviting school. Our school counselors will conduct

an at-risk awareness workshop for all staff so they can better implement intervention procedures for potential dropouts. We will also have an invitational brainstorming session with the faculty during this program to create more ways to invite school success.

What Advice Would You Offer New Implementers of Invitational Learning?

The implementation of the Invitational Learning model in our school was greatly facilitated when we decided to adopt it as our philosophy. In addition, our success has been based on a strong commitment to teamwork.

In contrast, I observed a high school in another state where efforts to improve student success were also plentiful. Businesses were involved and the administrator was highly motivated, dynamic and skilled in public relations. Despite these positive ingredients, teacher feedback at this school suggested a lack of involvement and ownership of the good things that were happening. "Yes, we go along for the ride," one teacher admitted, "but we never really know what's coming up next." At East Davidson High, teachers know what is coming up because they design it, plan it, and implement it.

The philosophy committee that originally investigated the possibility of a new school philosophy was also a good place to start. My advice for anyone who wants to implement Invitational Learning is to begin by creating an atmosphere of acceptance. See your faculty and students as able, valuable, and responsible, and let them taste the flavors of cooperative, collegial decision making.

Support for Invitational Learning follows naturally because the basic concepts and beliefs are proactive, positive and beneficial to all concerned. The approach is one of self-concept development, which means it enhances the vital relationship between human perception and behavior. If faculty and students see themselves as integral parts of a dynamic system, they will become motivated and involved in positive directions. With such unanimous participation, everyone shares pride in the results.

At East Davidson High, teachers know what is coming up because they design it, plan it, and implement it.

My advice for anyone who wants to implement Invitational Learning is to begin by creating an atmosphere of acceptance.

Chapter 9

The Kansas Elementary School Curriculum Experience

John H. Wilson

What Attracted You to the Invitational Learning Model?

As an elementary teacher educator, curriculum consultant, writer of elementary materials, and presenter of numerous elementary education in-service programs, my professional responsibilities center on the elementary school curriculum. My orientation to elementary education is grounded in the conviction that a child's entire experiential being, while under the auspices of the school, must be attended and nurtured to assure that child's greatest advantage. My "dispositional set," to reference John Dewey, focuses elementary educators' responsibility to assure maximum mental, social, emotional, physical, and spiritual development for every child, with every opportunity, using all resources imaginable.

I first encountered the invitational education model in a little book, *Inviting School Success* (Purkey, 1978), some ten years ago, and was immediately drawn to the language of Invitational Learning. Conceptualizing the basic precepts, elements, and beliefs of Invitational Learning offered a sensible way to organize my professional thinking. Recent happenings in American schools and their responses to the many-faceted pressures brought to bear by national reports on the state of education have convinced me that Invitational Learning makes even more sense today, and deserves serious study.

My early identification with Invitational Learning was enormously gratifying as I discovered many professional

Conceptualizing the basic precepts, elements, and beliefs of Invitational Learning offered a sensible way to organize my professional thinking.

allies and friends who were also aligned with the beliefs of Invitational Learning. The lucid explanations about the power of invitations to help correct the rather jaundiced state of American schooling were soothing music to my ears.

Three decades of being a participant/observer/student in elementary education curriculum have forced the personal realization that our schools are losing sight of the relative importance of children's affective development. Pressures to improve children's cognitive competence have increased, partly as a result of the many investigations and resulting reports about the condition of schools and schooling. And, while they are certainly not mutually exclusive movements, **intentional** affective education curricula in my opinion has been diminished while the cognitive competence thrust has been rewarded.

...our schools are losing sight of the relative importance of children's affective development.

My observations include increasing evidence that schools and teachers are buckling under the pressures to "return to the basics," raise achievement test scores, and teach primarily for critical/analytical/problem-solving thinking skills. Teachers report to me the sense of pressure, tension, and obligation regarding this increased interest in "accountability" to meet arbitrary standards, often mandated by those not intimate with children's social, psychological, physical, and educational needs.

Elkind (1981) speaks about these, "hurried children (who) seem to make up a large portion of the troubled children seen by clinicians today; they constitute many of the young people experiencing school failure, those involved in delinquency and drugs, and those who are committing suicide" (p.vii). Thus, to me, schools are less enjoyable places for too many children today and, just as important, my observations convince me that schools are less enjoyable places for far too many educators. If the "effective schools/back-to-basics" curricula are so defensible, then why am I seeing so much unhappiness, unrest, and discontent at the work/school site?

...schools are less enjoyable places for too many children today and...schools are less enjoyable places for far too many educators.

With particular consideration given to the broader concept definition of curriculum, aligning myself with Invitational Learning made sense. To begin with, Invitational Learning does not include a power struggle over which is more important, cognitive **or** affective development. Proponents of Invitational Learning point to the research that supports the thesis that when teachers give more attention to the affective component in curricula, students show greater gains in the cognitive domain. Attending, quite naturally, to children's affective needs results in greater overall performance and higher achievement test scores.

What Strategy Did You Use in Gaining Adoption of the Model?

My good fortune allows me to work with both pre-service and in-service elementary educators: classroom teachers, building level administrators, supervisors, counselors, and other personnel. I introduce each of these populations to Invitational Learning and extend the conceptualization of the concept and process to their personal lives if they are receptive. My experiences of introducing the model have included working with an entire school district, presenting to elementary school faculties, and communicating with individual educators.

As one might expect, the school district is making slow and sometimes imperceptible progress with the districtwide practice of Invitational Learning. Introducing the model, assessing the five P's—people, places, policies, programs, and processes, and converting a significant number of school district leaders is challenging. On the other hand, with individual elementary school faculties, I have observed significant positive responses to the model among teachers and students within a relatively short period of time. The effects of the conscientious practice of the model within a one-to-one personal relationship have been clearly identified in a day or two, or over a weekend. Thus, I invite all of my students to experiment with the basic tenets of Invitational Learning, both personally and professionally, and within more than one personal or professional setting.

Perhaps the group that gives me the most helpful feedback is my semester-long student teacher class. These budding professionals observe the practice of teaching within several domains: at the university with teacher educators, at the assigned school site with a cooperating teacher and other elementary educators, and as a practitioner with elementary students. Their introduction to Invitational Learning is tested on all fronts.

...when teachers give more attention to the affective component in curricula, students show greater gains in the cognitive domain.

I invite all of my students to experiment with the basic tenets of Invitational Learning, both personally and professionally....

...novices observe the level and nature of Invitational Learning being expressed by teacher educators while they continue in the role of learner.

Back on campus for half a day each week of the semester, these novices observe the level and nature of Invitational Learning being expressed by teacher educators while they continue in the role of learner. The basic elements of invitational education are critically examined during the introduction of the model, tested by experience, and contrasted as an alternative to other learning and teaching models. Time to discuss these various experiences and interpretations helps student teachers to conceptualize the process of inviting oneself and others, and contributes to their assessment of the advantages and limitations of Invitational Learning.

At the school site, within an assigned classroom, the student teacher observes experienced educators working with young learners, more or less invitationally, and notices such things as learner responses, classroom environment, achievement performance, and morale. The student teacher has some freedom to experiment with the ideas being introduced, often as a comparison with techniques (a style) employed by the experienced teacher(s). More often than not, what the student teacher observes is Invitational Learning at a successful level, albeit unintentional and inconsistent. But, the student teacher is now equipped with a filter, a mirror, a language for reflecting upon the daily activities being observed. When disinviting behaviors are practiced with the elementary students there is a more sensitive awareness about the probable consequences; the students' responses are keenly observed. The theory is being tested dozens of times every hour and these observation data begin to make more sense, generally leading to commitment to the beliefs of Invitational Learning.

On a personal one-to-one relationship level, the student teacher receives almost instant feedback from fluently extending invitations. The effects associated with operating personally as a positive significant other are clear and compelling. My student teachers report their most meaningful acquaintance with Invitational Learning when they consciously express the process with one other person.

The effects associated with operating personally as a positive significant other are clear and compelling.

In-service teachers, typically working on a graduate degree by taking evening classes, have "next day" access to elementary classes and begin their experimentation with the theory/basic beliefs/elements of the model as my course with them continues. A semester of comparing notes, sharing experiences, processing questions, and reporting progress encourages these teachers to carefully examine the claims made by this model.

How Does the Invitational Model Function in Your School?

A few examples of curriculum activities that complement the invitational model will serve to illustrate how teachers apply these beliefs in practice. For example, in one language arts class a teacher encouraged the students to create a school newsletter. This newsletter enabled students to use their emerging journalistic skills and also enhanced the school climate by improving communication.

A math teacher opened a "Quik Shoppe" in the classroom with play money as currency. She arranged for students to earn money by taking responsibilities in the classroom and to purchase privileges (perhaps some services) that the class thought were appropriate. Success of a venture such as the Quik Shoppe relies heavily on ideas and suggestions from students, and also emphasizes their management skills.

Another example of Invitational Learning is to have students practice oral history in social studies by interviewing senior citizens from the neighborhood or in their own families. A common set of questions can be used in order to compare responses. The interviews might lead to the insight that a particular geographical area has a unique integrity of its own. The results can also be compared with current social trends in the community.

Another example of Invitational Learning is to have students practice oral history in social studies by interviewing senior citizens....

Students can be invited to role play a character from a favorite book, dress up to depict the person and then try to "sell" the book to the rest of the class. A student can present his or her "sales pitch" by acting out a compelling part of the story. These dramatic presentations can end with nominations to recognize outstanding performances: (1) Most Convincing Actor/Actress, (2) Most Original/Accurate Costume, (3) Greatest Sales Appeal, (4) Book Most Likely to be Read by Others.

The preceding examples are only a few of the many ways that instruction can complement Invitational Learning. Curriculum can be made appealing and relevant to all

Teachers, counselors and other educators are only limited by the boundaries of their own creativity and willingness to reach out to students.

students in countless ways. Teachers, counselors and other educators are only limited by the boundaries of their own creativity and willingness to reach out to students. By using the principles of Invitational Learning, teachers can add life to their presentations, hold student interest, and encourage positive student behaviors that contribute to better class-room management.

Expectations within the invitational classroom are viewed as what the students "get to do," not what they "have to do." The students are invited to work on a social studies unit project, complete a math assignment, take a spelling review quiz, or work on a reinforcer at home. They do not have to do these things. School work is presented as an opportunity, rather than as an obligation. My experience has been that elementary students soon learn to accept this rather simple change in language and this entirely different perspective about learning as a gift and a genuine opportunity.

In summary, these few examples of curriculum modifications and the ideas about classroom management represent the basic beliefs of Invitational Learning as they are expressed through a total elementary curriculum—all of the students' experiences. The classroom teacher, school counselor, administrator, and other educators who practice this model are sensitive to literally hundreds of daily opportunities to convey limitless invitations. Children are bombarded by the fluent and artful classroom teacher's signals and messages which convey the basic beliefs, elements, and commitment to Invitational Learning. They are elevated by the programs and services offered by counselors and other helpers, and they are invited to a celebration of their own learning by a school climate that has been established by administrators and other decision makers.

How Successful Has the Program Been to Date?

The teachers are dependably critical and not easily persuaded to take up another "bandwagon" idea out of the university. Skepticism is prominent and I genuinely welcome this tentativeness. Most of my in-service teachers find the basic principles of Invitational Learning complementary to their fundamental professional beliefs and the personal guidelines that reflect their commitment to children's self-concept development. They confess that the value of more artful, fluent, sensitive, intentional invitational teaching is that it is challenging, comforting, and meaningful. These educators especially appreciate the language of Invitational Learning because it helps them express how they are trying to satisfy some of the pressure to raise test scores, without abandoning their interest in children's positive self-appraisals. One teacher remarked, "it gives us common language to argue with!" The teachers often report a sense of relief that their efforts to attend to children's affective development is defensible, as they recognize the system generally does not reward the outlay of energy required to practice invitational education.

...the value of more artful, fluent, sensitive, intentional invitational teaching is that it is challenging, comforting, and meaningful.

For the most part, my experienced elementary educator-students applaud the model as a sensible enterprise for meeting the most generally accepted goals agreed upon for elementary school curriculum today. That they find aligning themselves with the model not only personally gratifying but professionally rewarding is often viewed as too good to be true.

What Plans and Goals Do You Contemplate for the Future?

As I have observed the academic curriculum in elementary schools being modified to represent greater challenges for younger children, e.g., kindergarten children being introduced to formal reading instruction that had been reserved for first graders, and the consequent diminishing of time for "play" in the primary grades, I am moved to resist this trend. Elementary schools today seem to me to no longer be fun places. They are too serious and almost factory-like. They are not enjoyable and relaxing places to be. I see far too many children struggling with the rigors of "academe" in the early years of schooling, and subsequently being identified as "slow," "disabled," or pronounced incapable of handling the elementary curriculum.

Elementary schools today seem to me to no longer be fun places. They are too serious and almost factory-like.

My plans remain firm: I will continue the implementation of Invitational Learning throughout the elementary school curriculum. I will take advantage of every opportunity to connect elementary curriculum with Invitational Learning so that students will make the school their first choice on the list of the places they like to spend time.

My work with my own colleagues at the university has been richer, more meaningful, clearer, and more productive as I have conceptualized the model. Filtering my work through a clearer understanding of, and appreciation for, Invitational Learning has led me to believe that my efforts are indeed important and that my responsibilities as an elementary teacher educator can be fulfilled with greater, more positive, long-term effects. The model works for me, at several sites, with several constituencies, both personally and professionally, with varying degrees of success. My success increases in proportion to my investment of sensitivity and energy.

What Advice Would You Offer to New Implementers of Invitational Learning?

Classroom management is perhaps the most critical element in the elementary school curriculum to assure compliance with the invitational model. The process by which classroom teachers manage instruction and student behavior clearly delineates the central, primary value of the curriculum. Invitational classroom management operates from a perspective that firm but reasonable expectations for students' behaviors will lead to more independent and responsible choices and practices. Teachers set the tone with expectations that are typically higher than those embraced by most elementary students for themselves. This tone is positive and encouraging. Teachers involve students in identifying the behavioral limits in class and the consequences of exceeding them, and these standards become "ours" as opposed to "the teacher's" or "the school's." Students are urged to take ownership for these appropriate expectancies.

Successful invitational classroom management evolves out of a teacher's faith in the students and a genuine conviction that children can manage themselves, can learn to handle freedom and can become more responsible as they accept more responsibilities.

Successful invitational classroom management evolves out of a teacher's faith in the students and a genuine conviction that children can manage themselves....

Classroom management in the invitational classroom urges students to become skillful and responsible decision-makers by introducing the skills they need to identify alternate behaviors and to learn the consequences of these alternative paths. This is a time that teachers and school counselors can collaborate to intentionally help students become more effective decision makers, especially about issues that have significant personal and social impact. Invitational teachers and counselors believe that students will make intelligent, fair, and practical decisions as they recognize more than one or two ways to respond to challenges and temptations. The ability to accurately predict the consequences of one's behaviors is a valued skill that proves useful for a lifetime. It is a skill that can be learned in classroom instruction and in helping relationships with the school counselor.

My advice to educators who are less familiar with the model is to consider my own journey. Begin with *Inviting School Success* (Purkey & Novak, 1984), move into the experimentation stage, find a confidant or two with whom to share your experiences, turn to additional resources cited in this publication, attend an Invitational Education conference, and then carefully observe how the tenets of Invitational Learning can offer you the kind of professional and personal growth you value most.

...find a confidant or two with whom to share your experiences....

Chapter 10

The Affton School District Experience

Gary C. Benedict

What Attracted the Affton School District to the Invitational Learning Model?

Are you looking for a way to draw your community and schools together into a partnership to create excellent schools? Do you see a need to help individuals raise their expectations of their schools, their community, and themselves? Are you disturbed by a high suspension rate, high percentages of D and F grades, and resultant dropout rates? Are your concerns compounded by a desegregation program, building program, and a divided community, staff, or school board? You are not alone. These and other issues all too commonly confront boards of education, administrators, teachers, staff, and communitities. The Affton School District in suburban St. Louis, Missouri was confronting all of these issues by the mid 1980s.

The Affton School District had a reputation for almost 130 years as a sound school system, but recent events had eroded this long-time community partnership and vision. By the end of the 1986-87 school year, the district chose to seek new leadership and a nationwide search for a superintendent began.

As the new superintendent, I reviewed the community and school needs assessment that had taken place prior to the superintendent search. Several goals to address the community's needs were tentatively identified:

- Raise the aspirations of the school, the community and each individual.

Are you looking for a way to draw your community and schools together into a partnership to create excellent schools?

- Develop a partnership among the home, school, and community.
- Assure that all students regardless of race, sex, or socio-economic conditions reach their full potential.

As I reviewed these objectives, I realized that the Invitational Learning model was the ideal approach to use in leading this community and school system. My first encounter with Invitational Learning had occurred a few years before in Wisconsin when I attended an educational conference as an IDEA fellow. At that conference, the keynote address was delivered by Professor William Watson Purkey. In his remarks, Dr. Purkey spoke about how we can make school the "most inviting place in town" and how important it is that everyone in schools—students, parents, teachers and other staff—be considered valuable, capable, and accountable in the learning process.

Dr. Purkey spoke about how we can make school the "most inviting place in town"...

In my first address to the staff of the Affton School District, I foreshadowed themes to come as I advised "You cannot sell from an empty cart." I emphasized the tremendous need for a positive self-image for students and staff. Strategies were presented to empower teachers and all staff to begin to recognize and affirm the positive characteristics of each other, thus providing the foundation and model for a more positive approach to dealing with students and learning.

What Strategies Were Used in Gaining Acceptance and Adoption of the Invitational Learning Model?

Several strategies were identified to help the district achieve its goals and help the schools and community regain their vision:

- Introduction of the philosophy of Invitational Learning.
- Establishment of a *Goals for Greatness* committee to develop a long-range plan for the district.
- Use of the effective school's research/characteristics as a consistent yardstick for evaluating policies, practices and results.
- Establishment of an organized system to provide for collaborative processes.

- Review of discipline practices.
- Development of a community education program.

Early in the 1987-88 school year, Dr. John Novak, co-author of *Inviting School Success* (Purkey & Novak, 1984), addressed the Affton School District staff. Parents, board members, citizens, and other school districts were invited to attend, both to build a consensus that schools ought to be places which are inviting to students, parents and staff and to begin collaborative processes. In this meeting of the community, Dr. Novak stressed common values regarding the education of all children and the importance of schools creating environments and processes by which all students can feel valuable, capable, and responsible.

Following this presentation, an organized system was initiated to encourage collaborative processes across the Affton School District:

- Parent Advisory Committees and Teacher Advisory Committees were established at each school.
- A District Instructional Improvement Committee was formed.
- Building Site Committees comprised of neighbors and parents were established.
- A Staff Development Committee, including representatives of all employee groups, was established.
- An Administrative Council composed of all administrators was established.

Work began promptly to utilize the committee structure to hammer out a district Philosophy of Education.

A districtwide *Goals for Greatness Committee* was established and representatives drawn from all of the committees. Additional nominations of members were solicited to represent parent organizations, private school parents, senior citizens, the Affton Board of Education, the teacher's union, and the Chamber of Commerce. A series of evening meetings began where teachers, parents, and citizens recreated their common vision of a future for the school system.

A district *Discipline Committee* was also established to address the issue of creating safe and orderly schools and the need to make schools more inviting. In January of 1988 the superintendent of schools charged this district *Discipline Committee*, composed of teachers, counselors and administrators with the mission of recommending a K-12 discipline policy. The proposed policy was to incorporate:

- The Philosophy of Education adopted by the Board of Education,
- The philosophy and concepts of Invitational Learning,
- The research on self-concept, reward, and punishment,
- The manner in which we would want our own children treated, and a plan to reduce suspensions and dropout rates.

To accomplish this mission, the committee reviewed the current *Discipline Guidelines* in Affton schools, studied the state guidelines, discussed a variety of discipline models, and reviewed the available research on positive discipline, self-concept, reward, and punishment. The committee also hosted a working session with Dr. David Strahan of the University of North Carolina at Greensboro, co-author of *Positive Discipline: A Pocketful of Ideas* (Purkey & Strahan, 1986), which is based on Invitational Learning. The committee formulated a draft of *Discipline Guidelines*, which was submitted to the superintendent for discussion and action by the Superintendent's Cabinet and the Administrative Council.

A revised draft of the guidelines was reviewed by the Parent Advisory Committee at each school, the school law section of the Department of Elementary and Secondary Education, Special School District, and legal counsel. The Board of Education formally approved a final draft of the *Student Discipline Guidelines* in June of 1988.

At the opening of the 1988–89 school year copies of the *Student Discipline Guidelines* were distributed to each staff member, mailed to the parents of all students, and provided for all students in grades 6–12.

A number of strategies are being used to make the Affton schools inviting places for students, parents and staff.

How Does the Invitational Model Function in the Affton Schools?

A number of strategies are being used to make the Affton schools inviting places for students, parents and staff.

Collaborative Processes to Build Partnership and Self-worth. Affton uses committees to invite everyone into the educational partnership. The committees were formed realizing that the decision-making process should involve those people affected by the decision itself. Committee members were encouraged to solicit a range of comments, concerns and ideas.

Superintendent's Advisory Councils; Administrative Council and Teacher Advisory Council. These groups aim to provide staff members with an opportunity to communicate directly with the superintendent. They advise the superintendent on how they think the decision-making process is or is not working. Each committee/council presents items to the superintendent for review; the superintendent then gives his recommendations to the various committees.

Building-Level Teacher Advisory Committees. These committees give those affected by decisions at the building level input to the principal. They are building-level improvement committees aimed at creating excellent, effective, and inviting schools. The committee's work should result in increased attendance, decreased suspensions and dropouts, increased achievement, and a larger percentage of students continuing their education. These committees help to ensure that building-level decisions reflect the building's human and financial limitations. They review items referred to them by the principal and administration.

Instructional Improvement Council. This council reviews proposals for curriculum changes. It is charged with creating effective and inviting schools across the district, and assuring that the changes are within the human and financial limitations of the district. It is charged with developing, implementing and maintaining a long-range plan for curriculum and coordination and improvement. The council also aligns exit and enabling expectations with tests used. Schools should test what is taught and teach what is to be tested. To do this, the Affton schools align what is expected of students at the end of a grade with the standardized tests to be used. Enabling expectations, unit or lesson goals, should align with student exit expectations and with the formative tests, quizzes, and other measures of student performance. The Instructional Improvement

Schools should test what is taught and teach what is to be tested....the Affton schools align what is expected of students at the end of a grade with the standardized tests to be used.

Council reviews items referred by the assistant super-intendent for curriculum and personnel.

Staff Development Committee. This committee identifies the staff development needed to create effective and inviting schools and is charged with developing a long-range plan for all employee groups. Some areas the committee will examine are: an employee wellness program; orientation for new employees; professional development programs for new and veteran teachers; first-aid training for volunteers, coaches, secretaries and others; and training related to communicable diseases and sanitation.

Pupil Services Committee. This committee provides input to the director of pupil services. It has been charged with developing student wellness and programs for students who are at risk of school failure.

Building Site Committees. These committees give community members a voice in decisions which affect their neighborhoods, aesthetically or in regard to recreational opportunities. They provide input to the business manager and director of buildings and grounds. The committees review items referred by the business manager and/or administration, and work on developing a long-range plan for site improvements.

Building-Level Parent Advisory Committees. These committees are established at each building and are comprised of parents who communicate with the principal. They are working to increase attendance, decrease suspensions and dropouts, increase achievement, and encourage all students to continue their education. They review items referred to them by the principal or administration.

Parent Advisory Committees have discussed a variety of issues. Parents have heard and responded to the district's newly developed Philosophy of Education. They also reviewed the Student/Parent Handbook and recommended some changes. The discipline plan and suspension guidelines were discussed by these committees. Parents were able to review the homework policy and the grade reporting system.

Awards and Recognition to Enhance Self-Esteem and School Spirit. A second component of the inviting school model used in Affton is frequent awards and recognition to encourage success. Research has shown the powerful effects of positive reinforcement in the learning process. The research on effective schools has identified frequent awards and recognition as an important characteristic of successful schools.

As Affton looked at the situation and considered the evidence, the question remained, "How can a district, in an organized way, use these powerful concepts to help **all** students learn more, better, faster?" The school district has devised the following three awards:

Cougar Team: Districtwide recognition for students whose achievement scores equal or exceed projected scores based on their ability.

A-Team: Districtwide recognition for students who have earned a composite achievement score greater than 90 percent of the students nationally who take the same standardized test.

Gold Team: Districtwide recognition for students who have earned a grade point average of "B" or better for the first semester of the school year.

Award winners receive a certificate and participate in a drawing for prizes which are donated by the community. These include sandwiches, savings bonds, free bowling and other prizes. Winners are entitled to purchase team shirts exclusive to award winners. All profits from shirt sales go to the Affton Youth Fund, a source for purchasing future prizes.

An Outcome-Based Curriculum for Student Success. During the 1987-88 school year, the *Instructional Improvement Committee* was hard at work with school counselors and administrators developing a five-year plan for the orderly review of all components of the district's program. The committee reviewed the district philosophy, characteristics of effective schools, and data about the state of district programs to create a five-year plan which will result in a coordinated, closely aligned curriculum. The committee's mission was to create a program where students learned better and faster, where all students regardless of race, sex or socio-economic condition reach their full potential.

The research on effective schools has identified frequent awards and recognition as an important characteristic of successful schools.

The Goals of Greatness Committee...identified the need for an improved guidance and counseling program if the district was to be successful in achieving its goals.

The *Goals of Greatness Committee* met and reviewed community surveys, demographics, and the district's Philosophy of Education. Early in their deliberations, they identified the need for an improved guidance and counseling program if the district was to be successful in achieving its goals. Meanwhile, the *Instructional Improvement Committee* was reaching a similar conclusion.

Simultaneously, the Missouri State Department of Education offered comprehensive guidance program grants to assist districts in the development, implementation, and evaluation of a comprehensive, systematic guidance and counseling program. The Affton School District applied to the State Department of Education and received one of these grants.

Self-Studies for School Improvement. During the 1988-89 school year, a self-study committee of parents, teachers, counselors, and administrators worked collaboratively to develop recommendations. Committee members reviewed the school district philosophy, participated in sessions for implementing the comprehensive guidance model, studied the state of the art in guidance and counseling, examined time and task analyses completed by district school counselors, and sought input from staff, parents, and students through a series of needs surveys. The committee reviewed and recommended a Board of Education Policy of Guidance and Counseling and a Philosophy for a School Counseling Program. The committee synthesized the data and formulated a comprehensive developmental guidance program that emphasizes the introduction, reinforcement and mastery of specific concepts and appropriate age levels.

The work of the *Guidance and Counseling Committee* was submitted to the *Instructional Improvement Committee* and sent forward with a recommendation to the Administrative Council. The Council reviewed the report and made its recommendation to the superintendent who made his recommendation for adoption to the board. Modifications based on the committee's report are being made, and a schedule for future program implementation and evaluation has been adopted.

How Successful Has the Invitational Learning Model Been to Date?

In the Affton schools the implementation of Invitational Learning has resulted in a number of positive outcomes. These include:

- A clearer instructional focus for the district based on proceedings of Administrative Council meetings, self-study committees, and Board of Education policies and instructional recommendations.
- More students are receiving awards and recognition.
- Teacher morale has increased.
- For the first time in its 130 year history, Affton won the region in three out of four fall sports, including an undefeated football team.
- Total fourth-grade composite achievement test scores exceeded the projected scores of students based on ability.
- Fourth-grade tuition transfer student's composite achievement scores also exceeded their projected scores based on ability.
- Seventh-grade ability scores show that Affton has more students in the upper half and upper quartile than occurs nationally, and more students scored in the top quartile on achievement than in ability test results.
- The percentage of resident parents choosing Affton High School increased this fall. Again this year, the percentage of kindergarten parents indicating they will send their child to first grade in the Affton schools has increased to the largest percentage ever.
- Results of a survey indicates that the *Student Discipline Guidelines*:

  1. Sends a clear message;
  2. Reflects the philosophy of the district and the basic concepts of Invitational Learning;
  3. Incorporates the key components of effective schools;

More students are receiving awards and recognition. Teacher morale has increased.

4. Meets the requirement of the Excellence in Education Act that each school district develop a policy on discipline;
5. Assists in the reduction of out-of-school suspensions.

During the 1987-88 school year, there were 200 out-of-school suspensions in the Affton School District. The *Student Discipline Guidelines* were implemented in the beginning of the 1988-89 school year and as of March 31, 1989 there have been 69 out-of-school suspensions.

We have been further pleased with the results of numerous parent surveys and comments supporting the current restructuring efforts.

What Plans and Goals Do You Contemplate for the Future?

The Affton School District is in the process of moving toward a pluralistic, collegial concept of organization. Committees have been established to provide for a pluralistic sharing of power to make program recommendations on a collegial basis.

We believe a clear school mission is one of the key elements of effective and inviting schools.

We intend to continue to focus our efforts to implement the district's Philosophy of Education. We believe a clear school mission is one of the key elements of effective and inviting schools. That mission statement, or philosophy, is the measuring stick for all of the district's policies and decisions.

The philosophy provides the cornerstone for developing our long-range plan: *Goals for Greatness*. Our long-range plan is built on this philosophy of education and what we know about effective learning and inviting schools.

Affton school board members, educators, parents, students, and citizens are working to implement our district's long-range plan, which encompasses all the factors of Invitational Learning: people, places, policies, programs, and processes. All these elements coexist and must blend together in a mosaic that provides for quality and promotes excellence in education.

What Advice Would You Offer to New Implementers of Invitational Learning?

In applying the invitational approach in a system-wide school effort these suggestions may be helpful:

1. Adopt a philosophy of education that reflects current community values. Review the philosophy on an annual basis and revise as needed.
2. Provide development opportunities for all students, parents, and teachers to learn about effective and inviting schools.
3. Establish broad-based committees, which include professional staff and parents, and invite them to grow both personally and professionally as they make their schools more inviting and effective for students.
4. Give committees a mission statement that makes clear the purpose and direction of their efforts.
5. Develop a philosophy of guidance and counseling for your school district, which embraces the idea that every educator, teacher, parent, and counselor plays a significant role in the enhancement of student self-concept.
6. Examine the state of the art. Compare your programs to state of the art programs and identify strengths and weaknesses based on the evidence. Make clear, reasonable, and reachable recommendations for change.
7. Establish goals and objectives that are observable, measurable, and do-able.

Adopt a philosophy of education that reflects current community values.

Make clear, reasonable, and reachable recommendations for change.

Chapter 11

The University of South Carolina Adjunct Instructor Experience

Cheryl French Stehle

What Attracted You to the Invitational Education Model?

During the late 1970's while completing an administrative internship in a school system in upstate New York, the associate superintendent of schools, the director of pupil personnel services, and I met with counseling personnel at a local high school. The principal of this high school began to tell us about a leadership conference he had recently attended. He was obviously excited about what he had heard at this conference and this excitement was reflected in his enthusiastic summary of a presentation given by a university professor from Florida.

"This guy," the principal exclaimed, "has the idea that our schools should be the most inviting places in town. It's been a long time since I've heard a speaker who could so powerfully move an audience—especially an audience of secondary school principals." The principal continued his unqualified endorsement, saying "We need to get this fellow up here to talk to staff throughout the county."

At that moment the associate superintendent turned to me and suggested that as part of my administrative internship, I should continue to work with the committee in charge of in-service training and look into the possibility of having this motivational speaker join us for our next staff development conference. When I called this professor, he had another engagement on our first in-service date, but we eventually scheduled him to visit upstate New York.

"This guy," the principal exclaimed, "has the idea that our schools should be the most inviting places in town."

*..."human poten-
tial...is there
waiting to be
discovered and
invited forth."*

The professor was William Watson Purkey, and more than a decade has passed since I first heard him speak about Invitational Learning. Nevertheless, I vividly recall the impact he had on the audience. The staff enthusiastically applauded Dr. Purkey's message that "human potential, while not apparent, is there waiting to be discovered and invited forth."

Later in 1979 during my doctoral studies, a professor loaned me a copy of the classic in perceptual psychology, the 1962 ASCD yearbook, *Perceiving, Behaving, Becoming.* While reading this monumental book I heard the "big click" and the wonder of synthesis unfolded. Suddenly, links were formed and relationships established.

In my work I had been focusing on the development of curriculum and was especially attracted to research concerning achievement in reading. Not surprisingly, reading achievement was closely associated with positive attitudes toward reading and those attitudes tended to enhance the habit of reading. Simply stated, when students exhibited a good attitude about reading, they tended to read more frequently; this in turn enhanced achievement test scores. None of this seemed out of place. My question, however, concerned the "positive attitude" aspect of reading success. The theory seemed to have merit but how was one to foster a "positive reading attitude?" Bridging the gap between theory and practice became the issue and at this point the research question for my dissertation was discovered. I decided to explore the formation of positive attitudes and their link to good reading habits, which would in turn result in higher levels of reading achievement.

Arthur W. Combs had been concerned with the positive view of the self and with acceptance (i.e., "the person in the process"); after reading some of his writings, I turned to another author who also was associated with the University of Florida—William Watson Purkey.

After reading *Self-Concept and School Achievement* (Purkey, 1970), I discovered a later book by Purkey, *Inviting School Success: A Self-Concept Approach to Teaching and Learning* (1978), and found Invitational Learning. Suddenly, many pieces of the puzzle concerning the link between achievement and attitude began to fall into place.

*Suddenly, many
pieces of the
puzzle concerning
the link between
achievement and
attitude began to
fall into place.*

My original concern focused on reading achievement and I had been researching the Sustained Silent Reading programs (SSR), a supplement to traditional basal test approaches. Sustained Silent Reading programs structure a period of silent, uninterrupted reading for all students. Everyone in the class, including the teacher, reads silently until the end of the SSR period.

My initial response to SSR had been negative, but as I implemented the program I was impressed with the results. SSR did seem to be working. Students were actually enjoying reading and this was a step in the right direction. If youngsters enjoyed reading, they would surely develop a positive attitude toward reading and this would foster better reading habits that would result in higher achievement. All of this seemed relatively simple and certainly made sense, yet one question remained: Why does SST work? When I examined the program in depth, I found within the SSR supplemental reading program a framework for Invitational Learning. Students were reading because they were responding to the powerful positive messages of a program that was "intentionally inviting."

I was excited about the implications for utilizing Invitational Learning in academic areas (across all grade levels) and beyond the school environment into medicine, health care, and all of the helping professions (e.g., counseling and nursing). Teacher education was only the beginning. Invitational Learning serves as a paradigm for all of the helping professions. The possibilities for relationships, personal and professional, are limitless.

Students were reading because they were responding to the powerful positive messages of a program that was "intentionally inviting."

What Strategy Did You Use in Gaining Adoption of the Model?

During my doctoral studies I began to focus on specific factors that made SSR successful. I wanted to find out why it worked as well as it did. As I closely examined each facet of the process, it became clear that messages such as those embraced by Invitational Learning were fundamental to the success of the SSR approach.

The SSR program had been mandated by the local school system and not surprisingly some teachers had sabotaged the program by simply going through the motions. I too had negative perceptions toward SSR when it was first introduced. "Just another add-on program," I thought, "in a curriculum already too complex."

When I began to see positive results (e.g., better attitudes toward reading, the development of good reading habits, and increased success in reading test scores), my original response ("This is a waste of time.") turned to a growing, but guarded, enthusiasm for the program ("Perhaps this is a worthwhile effort after all."). This change in perception coincided with my discovery of Invitational Learning, which I began to implement within the SSR program. This was done in my own classes, but occasionally I shared by experiences with teachers in our department at the high school. At the conclusion of my dissertation, which linked the SSR program to a positive, humanistic atmosphere where children are invited to become actively involved in a shared learning experience, I noted the essential relationship between successful implementation of SSR and Invitational Learning. I also identified potential roadblocks to the acceptance and implementation of instructional approaches such as the SSR program.

One major concern I identified centered on the lack of in-service training available to faculty in implementing new programs. To maximize success, it was suggested that staff development opportunities incorporate the concepts and processes presented in the invitational education model.

In the years since my work with the SSR program I have applied Invitational Learning to my work as an educational consultant and my teaching at the university level. In these experiences I have discovered that a major strategy for encouraging others to accept and adopt the invitational approach is through my own modeling of the practice. I have found that a key element in getting students and teachers to embrace Invitational Learning is in my own practice of the principles and beliefs of inviting relationships. As a professor and educational consultant, it is more important that I reflect the hallmarks of Invitational Learning than it is to simply tell about its assumptions and philosophy. By modeling these beliefs in my personal and professional relationships, I am able to illustrate both the "what" and the "how" of Invitational Learning.

...a major strategy for encouraging others to accept and adopt the invitational approach is through... modeling of the practice.

How Does the Model Function in Your Unit?

The invitational model functioned well at the secondary level when applied to the SSR program. Specifically, the implementation of the model made a good program better. The model embraces the notion that the more explicit the invitation, the better chance it has of being recognized. With this in mind, SSR students were "invited" to experience success in reading.

Now that I am teaching undergraduate and graduate students at the university, I find that Invitational Learning can be applied successfully across a wide audience—young college freshmen through older graduate students. In my role as a college instructor I make every attempt to establish both personal and professional relationships that reflect invitational principles and practices. For example, on the personal level I greet students as they enter the class every night. By shaking hands, using student names as you speak to them, and asking them about themselves you create a positive, accepting environment. When possible, I provide a snack for the first class meeting. This personal touch is greatly appreciated by graduate students who teach school all day or have other employment and then come to an evening class. Sometimes I will suggest that we take turns preparing a treat to be shared with everyone during the class break. When this is put to a vote, the results have always been positive.

On one occasion we held the final class meeting of a graduate seminar at a student's home. Everyone brought a dish to share and we had a pot-luck supper. After dinner we held class on the screened porch, enjoying the early spring breezes that came across the Port Royal Sound. It was a most delightful way to celebrate our final meeting and reflect on what we had accomplished over the semester.

Professionally, the invitational principles can also be applied in a variety of ways. In my teaching I have found that my **attitude** is an essential ingredient to my success. When I model a warm, positive and caring level of concern for the students and the subject matter, the class is successful. In particular, I exemplify the principles of Invitational Learning by arriving well prepared for class, setting reasonably high standards for students, encouraging active participation in class, and being a positive role model. One way to encourage student participation, for example, is to send personal thank you notes when students have spoken or given a class presentation. Our actions often speak louder than our words.

By shaking hands, using student names as you speak to them, and asking them about themselves you create a positive, accepting environment.

How Successful Has the Program Been to Date?

The research on the application of Invitational Learning with the SSR program showed that it was highly successful. Of the 200 students who answered six open-ended essay questions, approximately 92 percent expressed positive attitudes toward the SSR program.

Teacher responses were somewhat less positive, but still confirmed a belief in the value of the project. The teacher responses were further explained as feelings of frustration, which included concerns about insufficient details and materials and a lack of in-service opportunities.

I am pleased to say that my continuing use of Invitational Learning as an educational consultant and university instructor has harvested positive results with a wide audience of students at the undergraduate and graduate levels. Of particular value to me, personally and professionally, are the comments students send about their experiences in class and their exposure to Invitational Learning. To illustrate, one student who completed two of my classes sent a card with the following message:

> Thank you for the gifts you gave me—the laughter, the love, and for being my friend.

To this the student added a touching comment:

> Your gifts are so very special: unconditional respect and love, friendship, hope for attaining goals and belief in your students. Thank you my friend.

These personal evaluations, combined with my research findings on Invitational Learning, encourage me to continue the quest for ways to develop people, places, policies, programs, and processes that will create beneficial educational and helping relationships. The more I learn about this approach and the more I apply it in my own professional practice, the more convinced I am of its usefulness over a wide range of educational and human endeavors.

What Plans and Goals Do You Contemplate for the Future?

I continue to be interested in student success in reading, and am now increasingly interested in the process of infusing Invitational Learning across the school curriculum. I believe we need to bridge the gap between theory and practice and be concerned about connecting with "disconnected" populations within our schools. This "reaching out" must also reflect allied professions such as nursing, counseling, social work, and others. We need to be **inclusive** rather than **exclusive**, and this translates into being intentionally inviting rather than allowing ourselves and our colleagues to slip into patterns that are harmful, destructive, and counterproductive to our educational mission.

...we need to bridge the gap between theory and practice and be concerned about connecting with "disconnected" populations within our schools.

My goal is to continue to artfully and dramatically invite students to become excited about their potential; to inspire them to believe in themselves as talented, capable and caring persons. In pursuing this goal, I try to practice what I preach and continue to model Invitational Learning. By believing in my students and demonstrating that belief via careful, purposeful action, I nurture their self-development, a primary focus of the invitational approach.

Each time I teach a class or present a seminar, I have the opportunity to sell Invitational Learning. This fall, for example, I plan to offer districtwide in-service workshops to teachers in our county. The beginning of a new school year is an ideal time for teachers, counselors and other educators to learn about Invitational Learning. I look forward to this opportunity.

Also, this fall I will offer a special course for graduate students that will focus entirely on the invitational model and the theories of Invitational Learning. I am excited about this new adventure and feel it would also make a marvelous workshop in an intensive one-week format during the following summer. It would be exciting to have teachers from across the state join us in the Low Country of South Carolina, famous for its hospitality, charm and relaxing atmosphere!

In areas outside of education I am also finding ways to apply the invitational approach. I have written articles for a regional magazine, and found the ideals of Invitational Learning helpful in expressing warmth, joy, celebration, and a sense of challenge to my audience. For example, when writing about a summer music festival, I invite readers to plan a picnic, celebrate the season, and enjoy a concert under the stars. In writing about these experiences and opportunities, I try to give more than simply the facts of who, what, when, where, how, and why. I extend an invitation to join in the celebration in much the same way the song "Some Enchanted Evening" invites us to "meet a stranger." This may sound like an "Auntie Mame" philosophy, but I have found the articles to be well received, and my invitations accepted!

What Advice Would You Offer to New Implementers of Invitational Learning?

It is not necessary to begin any new implementation of Invitational Learning on a large scale or schoolwide basis. Staff commitment need not involve all faculty members or even the majority of staff. Those who choose to implement the model, however, should do so in response to a belief in the basic fundamentals of invitational education.

A good beginning may grow from a small group of advocates who seek to model, both personally and professionally, the invitational approach. A modest start can grow into something much more dynamic as time passes. An important element to keep in mind is that success with Invitational Learning is more likely when we consistently and dependably include as many people as possible in this process of growing and learning. It is this consistency and dependability that defines the quality of intentionality in Invitational Learning. Intentionality gives our messages positive direction and purpose. Without this quality our behaviors lack consistency and dependability and threaten our credibility as teachers and helping professionals.

In this report I have emphasized that modeling is perhaps the most powerful way to initiate Invitational Learning. By modeling the principles and practices of the invitational approach we encourage others to perceive us as caring, competent professionals. Such modeling includes personally caring for ourselves so that we are better able to respond appropriately to the needs of others. At the same

Those who choose to implement the model...should do so in response to a belief in the basic fundamentals of invitational education.

time, it means behaving professionally in ways that optimize the functioning of those we hope to teach and help.

An enduring literary tradition has been the *carpe diem motif*: "seize the day" or "live for the moment." For new implementers of Invitational Learning beginnings can and perhaps should be modest. Seize the moment and start with yourself. Model the professionally inviting person, and then start sharing with your colleagues. As William Purkey reminds us, "Invitational Learning requires patience. The world was not created in a day, and neither are people."

Model the professionally inviting person, and then start sharing with your colleagues.

Chapter 12

The Sugar Loaf School Experience

Joel Blackburn

What Attracted You to Invitational Learning?

Much has been written about the decline of academic achievement in America's public schools during the last thirty years. Teachers and administrators across the nation are bombarded with report after report on how poorly our children perform in all academic areas when compared to children of other countries. This constant criticism of the educational system has led government decision makers to push for academic accountability with little attention focused on the emotional development of students.

Despite this alarming difference in measured achievement, many educators believe that our schools have accomplished far less in developing emotionally stable young people than in achieving academic competency. In practice, effective teaching and excellence in education should be based on respect for the welfare of the total student. In this regard, helping students develop emotional stability as well as intellectual advancement should be the creed of educators at all levels.

...effective teaching and excellence in education should be based on respect for the welfare of the total student.

I was drawn to Invitational Learning because of its focus on human dynamics and the mental health of everyone in schools. Each of the major assumptions of Invitational Learning focuses on attitudes as much as on methodology. Believing that all children are valuable, able and responsible creates a learning environment that nurtures the individual, establishes mutual respect, and lays the foundation for emotional steadfastness. These beliefs are the foundation for our teaching and helping relationships at Sugar Loaf School.

What Strategies Did You Use in Gaining Acceptance and Adoption of the Invitational Learning Model?

...the concept of intentionality provides a theoretical framework in which the school can choose strategies to become a beneficial presence in the lives of all students.

The belief of Invitational Learning that people can alter their attitudes and behaviors, combined with the positive concept of being personally and professionally inviting to oneself and others, is a powerful notion for schools and teachers. In addition, the concept of intentionality provides a theoretical framework in which the school can choose strategies to become a beneficial presence in the lives of all students. Intentional schools are visibly directed and purposeful in working towards their educational goals. For these schools, Invitational Learning is an excellent model because it offers a mind-set for teachers and students to consistently practice positive daily interactions with themselves and each other.

The first strategy promoted at Sugar Loaf School was the need of faculty and staff members to care for their own physical, social and emotional needs. By encouraging physical exercise, examining eating habits, and promoting the benefits of quiet time, we emphasized how essential appropriate self behaviors are to our ability to be helpful toward others. Consistent positive behavior toward oneself is a prerequisite to being able to help others.

This axiom also applies to how I, as instructional leader, function in the school. Being consistently professionally inviting toward the staff and faculty allows me the opportunity to model Invitational Learning for others. I approach each human interaction with the belief and the challenge that my response can foster a sense of caring and concern for other persons. Frequent individual conferences with teachers and monthly group conferences with teaching assistants gives us a vehicle to discuss concerns and implement strategies that ensure positive relationships for students and adults at our school. In addition, having attractive printed messages placed in the faculty lounge reminds us of the importance of examining our attitudes and motives when working with children.

One strategy we use to solicit the views and opinions of students, parents, faculty, and service personnel is through the *Inviting School Survey*. Reviewing the programs, policies, and physical surroundings of a school provides a realistic bench mark for determining the levels of awareness for an inviting philosophy. Identifying areas that need improvement provides the school with tangible points to begin creating an inviting climate.

How Does Invitational Learning Function in Your School?

Helping individual staff members practice an intentionally inviting philosophy is a primary task for me as administrator of the school. Faculty and staff constantly seek ways to improve the five P's—people, places, policies, programs, and processes—for Invitational Learning to experience progressive growth. As a result, our school has implemented a number of programs to help us maintain a wide-angle focus on achieving a healthy school climate. The following paragraphs describe a few of these efforts.

The school campus and physical plant are kept clean to encourage respect and teach responsible behavior. Home-rooms at Sugar Loaf School volunteer two days per month to pick up trash from the school grounds during physical education classes. This clean-up program teaches group cooperation and encourages pride in the campus. Sixth-grade students are assigned tasks to help with daily custodial duties. By sweeping hall rugs, cleaning mirrors, washing cafeteria tables, and carrying trash from the building, students accept responsibility and take pride in their school as well as in themselves. Student custodial care for the school activity bus has also been a successful strategy for building school pride.

A conscious effort is made to place attractive hanging baskets in hallways and living plants in classrooms to emphasize an environment of warmth and friendliness. Our PTA funded a landscaping project to replace unsightly shrubbery, and adult volunteers are planting new bushes and trees. We installed an enclosure around the trash dumpster and built wooden playground equipment for children of all ages to enjoy. The school cooperates with the local recreation association to keep the athletic field and playgrounds clean and in proper condition for safe play and enjoyment.

Believing that parents and grandparents are our greatest supporters, the teachers extend a continuous invitation for visitations to the classroom. Visiting school while children

The school campus and physical plant are kept clean to encourage respect and teach responsible behavior.

are involved in learning activities enables parents to better understand the curriculum and the goals of the teacher. Our school has gained many adult volunteers from first visits to classrooms where children were busily engaged in learning. Parents frequently take time from work to come for lunch with their children. Again, the reward for the school has been significant as parents are able to view the school in operation and judge for themselves the climate for learning.

All schools have rules to maintain order. Projecting rules as a means of establishing individual responsibility is the goal of our faculty. The school administration does not mandate a long list of rules, but instead entrusts teachers with the responsibility of establishing rules to ensure a comfortable learning environment in their classrooms. As the principal, I am involved with discipline practices and communicate my support to teachers through open dialogue and follow-up on all student referrals. Rules designed to promote maximum student safety in hallways, the cafeteria and gym, and on school buses are clearly stated and enforced fairly. School climate is enhanced when students believe that rules protect their right to a safe, nurturing learning environment.

School climate is enhanced when students believe that rules protect their right to a safe, nurturing learning environment.

Successful schools have an instructional program that meets the wide spectrum of needs and interests of the students they serve. Within the regular curriculum, all students experience success so that they develop a genuine feeling of self-worth. Teachers monitor the progress of students, building support for positive student involvement through success in the classroom. "Dignity Through Learning" is our school motto. It is our belief that children who know they can learn will demonstrate a strong positive self-image.

Honor roll field trips are provided at the end of each quarter for students in grades three through six. These opportunities encourage students to work for tangible rewards. At the same time, students are encouraged by their peers to strive for academic success. Parents become more involved in the academic activities of their children because of the immediate payback students receive from the honor roll recognition.

A program of academic intramurals has been implemented for students in grades four through six. This extra-curricular activity requires students to study math, science, language, social studies, vocabulary, music, and art for participation in a contest of quick recall based on the format of the television game show "Jeopardy." Participation has increased each year the contest has been offered, and students with a desire to excel in academics have been recognized for their efforts.

Attention to the five P's is essential if a school is to promote an image of growth as well as stability to the community. At Sugar Loaf School, we believe that the structure of the five powerful P's helps our school to create an instructional climate that is perceived as truly worthy of trust by students and parents.

How Successful Has Invitational Learning Been to Date at Your School?

Our faculty and staff have embraced the philosophy, goals and strategies of Invitational Learning. As educators, we are aware of the importance of being intentionally inviting with students, adults and colleagues, as well as with ourselves. We are also aware that the Invitational Learning is a continuous process. It is not simply doing one thing, establishing one program, or writing one policy. The invitational approach to helping relationships is multifaceted. It encourages teachers, counselors and administrators to choose and plan many avenues for improving schools and enhancing student development.

...Invitational Learning is a continuous process. It is not simply doing one thing, establishing one program, or writing one policy.

At Sugar Loaf School a majority of our certified staff has attended conferences sponsored by the International Alliance for Invitational Education. The faculty is encouraged to read books and periodicals about self-concept development and student achievement. These resources have been collected and catalogued in our professional library.

Our annual school goals reflect the importance of the affective development of all students. Throughout our instructional program we emphasize the value of each child as a unique person who has individual needs. This is a theme that teachers and I explore in our conferences and meetings during the year.

Our annual school goals reflect the importance of the affective development of all students.

Parent involvement has increased during our years of implementing Invitational Learning. Our parents realize that the adults who work with their children truly care about them. Involvement and commitment on the part of our parents have been rewarding to our teachers who appreciate the importance of parent support in establishing effective instructional programs and excellent schools.

Student discipline has also improved with fewer referrals to the principal's office. Peer influence has become an important component of helping students accept responsibility for their behavior. We have found that positive discipline is related to the students' acceptance of the school, their identification with its educational goals, and their belief that the school belongs as much to them as it does to anyone else.

What Plans and Goals Do You Contemplate for the Future?

Sugar Loaf serves many single parent families.... It is critical that we help single parents cope with the stress of parenting.

We believe it is important for our school to help parents develop effective parenting skills. Sugar Loaf serves many single parent families who feel the pressures of present day society. It is critical that we help single parents cope with the stress of parenting. In the future we plan "Family Night" workshops for parents to come to school and receive helpful suggestions for positive parent-child communication. In addition, parents and teachers will have the opportunity to talk to each other in an informal setting about general topics related to child development and learning.

In an attempt to address the dropout problem in our schools, each faculty member at Sugar Loaf School will "adopt" a high-risk student for the year. The adult will communicate with the student several times each week, both during school and after school hours, and will encourage student progress in school work and listen to the student's concerns. Our goal is to reach at-risk students at the primary and elementary school levels by providing positive, supportive relationships on a regular basis.

Our goal is to reach at-risk students...by providing positive, supportive relationships on a regular basis.

Additional emphasis will be given to our school's volunteer program by recruiting grandparents and other older citizens in the future. These adults offer a tremendous resource for our school. By inviting them to participate and contribute to our school program, we exemplify the wide-angle scope of Invitational Learning.

What Advice Would You Offer to New Implementers of Invitational Learning?

Schools that want to implement Invitational Learning should begin by soliciting volunteers from the faculty and parent community. In particular, the principal should identify and recruit teachers and other staff members who have the desire to perceive **all** students as special, capable and responsible people. If the school has a counselor and other helping professionals on staff, these persons should be included on the committee. This cadre of optimistic educators will become the guiding force in adopting and implementing the invitational approach.

A second, equally important step is for the principal to organize a committee to administrate the *Inviting School Survey*, study the results, and present the findings to the faculty and parents. Results of the survey provide a bench mark to assess Invitational Learning concepts within the context of a local school. The school can examine its people, places, policies, programs, and processes, and determine practical goals in implementing an invitational model.

Resources and books about Invitational Learning should be available in the school. Orientation and in-service for the entire faculty and staff should be provided throughout the year. All personnel should be involved in the implementation of Invitational Learning because, as the model emphasizes, everything and everyone counts. Nothing, and no one, is neutral in schools. All staff, including custodians, bus drivers, cafeteria workers, teaching assistants, and secretaries, should be informed and trained in the invitational approach. A truly inviting school exhibits positive relationships in all of its endeavors: the greeting students receive in the morning and the instruction they recieve during the day; visits to the school counselor; lunch in the cafeteria; recess on the playground; and a safe dismissal at the end of the day. Invitational Learning offers a refreshing global view of how schools can organize and create the most beneficial environments and deliver the most positive educational services for all students. In the process, they are able to keep a balanced focus on both academic achievement and personal, emotional development. For teachers, counselors and administrators, this balance is a hallmark of Invitational Learning.

All personnel should be involved in the implementation of Invitational Learning because...everything and everyone counts.

Conclusion

In this monograph we have presented the theory of Invitational Learning and examined its practical application across a variety of educational settings. The foundations, assumptions and processes espoused by Invitational Learning may at first seem simple, but their deeper meanings are sometimes difficult to grasp.

By focusing on the subtle but pervasive messages that exist in and around educational environments, this monograph has emphasized something familiar that has heretofore been largely overlooked: "You cannot miss the road to the City of Emerald, for it is paved with yellow brick." But Emerald Cities, like Invitational Learning, can sometimes be too obvious to see.

Four unhappy characters went to find the Wizard of Oz: a scarecrow who thought he had no brain, a tin woodsman who thought he had no heart, a lion who believed he had no courage, and a young girl who thought she lacked the power to make changes in her life. All were under the delusion that if they could only reach the Great and Terrible Wizard of Oz, he would grant them the things they sought. Little did they realize that they could do what they believed they could never do (kill the Wicked Witch of the West) and they returned to the Emerald City impatient for their rewards. There they discovered that wizards (like counselors) have no magic power.

Yet the Wizard did have marvelous powers to invite because he cared about people and believed certain things about them. To each of the four he sent a most powerful invitation: "A testimonial! A decree!" He invited them to see things in themselves that they had overlooked and to use what they already possessed. They had been looking in many strange and marvelous places for what was there all along—right in their own backyards.

Invitational Learning offers a pragmatic structure by which counselors and others can help people identify their

They had been looking in many strange and marvelous places for what was there all along—right in their own backyards.

119

...in a helping relationship, we can discover that most of the qualities we search for in life are found within ourselves.

capacity for a full, beneficial life. Successful counselors help people recognize that their silent, seemingly solitary searches for a heart, brain, courage, or direction in life are normal, human processes.

With the right mixture of ingredients in a helping relationship, we can discover that most of the qualities we search for in life are found within ourselves. Invitational Learning embraces this belief and relies on an optimistic, respectful, trustworthy, and intentional stance which considers a variety of environmental factors and human conditions to assist people in realizing their fullest potential. Stained glass is to sunshine what Invitational Learning is to counseling.

References

Amos, L. W. (1985). *Professionally and personally inviting teacher practices as related to affective course outcomes reported by dental hygiene students.* Unpublished doctoral dissertation, School of Education, University of North Carolina at Greensboro.

Antoine, D. S. E. (1943). *The little prince.* New York: Harcourt, Brace & World.

Carroll, L. (1949). *Alice in wonderland.* New York: Harper & Brothers.

Chandler, G. L. (1988). Invitational physical education. *Journal of Physical Education, Recreation, and Dance, 59*(4), 68–72.

Combs, A. W. (1972). Some basic concepts for teacher education. *The Journal of Teacher Education, 23,* 286–290.

Combs, A. W., Courson, C. C., & Soper, D. W. (1963). The measurement of self-concept and self-report. *Educational and Psychological Measurement, 23,* 493–500.

Combs, A. W., & Soper, D. W. (1963b). The perceptual organization of effective counselors. *Journal of Counseling Psychology, 10,* 222–227.

Combs, A. W., Soper, D. W., Gooding, C. T., Benton, J. A., Dickman, J. F., & Usher, R. H. (1969). Florida studies in the helping professions. *Social Science Monograph* (No. 37). Gainesville, FL: University of Florida Press.

Combs, A. W., Avila, D. L., & Purkey, W. W. (1971). *Helping relationships: Basic concepts for the helping professions.* Boston: Allyn & Bacon.

Combs, A. W., Avila, D. L., & Purkey, W. W. (1978). *Helping relationships: Basic concepts for the helping professions* (2nd ed.). Boston: Allyn & Bacon.

de Bono, E. (1986). *The CoRT thinking program* (2nd ed.). New York: Pergamon Press.

Durant, W. (1932). *On the meaning of life.* New York: Ray Long and Richard R. Smith, Inc.

Elkind, D. (1981). *The hurried child*. Reading, MA: Addison-Wesley.

Jourard, S. M. (1968). *Disclosing man to himself*. Princeton, NJ: Van Nostrand.

Jourard, S. M. (1971). *The transparent self: Self disclosure and well being* (rev. ed.). Princeton, NJ: Van Nostrand.

Hersey, P., & Blanchard, K. (1982). *Management of organizational behavior*. Englewood Cliffs, NJ: Prentice-Hall.

Ivey, A. E. (1986). *Developmental therapy*. San Francisco: Jossey-Bass.

Lehr, J. B., & Harris, H. W. (1988). *The at-risk low achieving student in the classroom*. Washington, DC: National Education Association.

Kelly, E. (1962). *Another look at individualism*. Detroit: Wayne State University, College of Education.

Little, J. W. (1982). Norms of collegiality and experimentation: Work place conditions and school success. *American Educational Research Journal, 19*(3), 325–340.

Maugham, W. S. (1944). *The razor's edge*. New York: Doubleday.

May, R. (1969). *Love and will*. New York: W. W. Norton & Co.

Mizer, J. E. (1964). Cipher in the snow. *NEA Journal, 53*, 8–10.

O'Roark, A. (1974). *A comparison of perceptual characteristics of elected legislators and public school counselors identified as most and least effective*. Unpublished doctoral dissertation, University of Florida, Gainesville.

Peck, M. S. (1978). *The road less traveled*. New York: Simon and Schuster.

Peters, T. J., & Waterman, R. H. (1982). *In search of excellence*. New York: Harper & Row.

Purkey, W. W. (1971). *Self concept and school achievement*. Englewood Cliffs, NJ: Prentice-Hall, Inc.

Purkey, W. W. (1978). *Inviting school success: A self-concept approach to teaching and learning*. Belmont, CA: Wadsworth Publishing Company.

Purkey, W. W. (1989). An overview of self-concept theory for counselors. *An ERIC/CAPS Digest*. Ann Arbor, MI: ERIC Counseling and Personnel Services Clearinghouse, University of Michigan.

Purkey, W. W., & Novak, J. M. (1984). *Inviting school success: A self-concept approach to teaching and learning* (2nd ed.). Belmont, CA: Wadsworth Publishing Co.

Purkey, W. W., & Novak, J. M. (1988). *Education: By invitation only.* Bloomington, IN: Phi Delta Kappa Educational Foundation.

Purkey, W. W., & Schmidt, J. J. (1982). Ways to be an inviting parent: Suggestions for the counselor-consultant. *Elementary School Guidance and Counseling, 17*(2), 94–99.

Purkey, W. W., & Schmidt, J. J. (1987). *The inviting relationship: An expanded perspective for professional counseling.* Englewood Cliffs, NJ: Prentice-Hall, Inc.

Purkey, W. W., & Stanley, H. (1989). *Connecting with the disconnected student: An invitational approach.* Greensboro, NC: Smith Reynold's Foundation Research Demonstration Project, University of North Carolina.

Purkey, W. W., & Strahan, D. B. (1986). *Positive discipline: A pocketful of ideas.* Columbus, OH: National Middle School Association.

Purkey, W. W., & Warters, R. (1986). Brass tack suggestions for the school executive. *Pennsylvania Schoolmaster, 18*(1), 6–8.

Ripley, D. M. (1986). Invitational teaching behaviors in the associate degree clinical setting. *Journal of Nursing Education, 25*(6), 240–246.

Rogers, C. (1951). *Client-centered therapy: Its current practice, implications, and theory.* Boston: Houghton Mifflin.

Rogers, C. (1967). *Coming into existence.* New York: World Publishing Co.

Rogers, C. (1974). In retrospect-forty-six years. *American Psychologist, 29,* 115.

Schmidt, J. J. (1982). Coordination and supervision of counseling services: An invitational approach. *Counselor Education and Supervision, 22*(2), 98–106.

Schmidt, J. J. (1988). *Invitation to friendship.* Minneapolis: Educational Media Corporation.

Sheehan, G. (1981). *This running life.* New York: Simon & Schuster.

Spikes, J. M. (1987). Invitational education: A model for nursing. *Nurse Educator, 12*(3), 26–29.

Strahan, D., & Strahan, J. (1988). *Revitalizing remediation in the middle grades: An invitational approach.* Reston, VA: National Association of Secondary School Principals.

Suls, J., & Greenwald, A. (Eds.). (1983). *Psychological perspectives on the self* (Vol. 2). Hillsdale, NJ: Erlbaum.

Wilson, J. (1986). *The invitational elementary classroom.*
Springfield, IL: Charles C. Thomas Publishers.
Wrenn, G. (1973). *The world of the contemporary counselor.* Boston: Houghton Mifflin.

Appendix A

The Inviting School Survey

William W. Purkey and James O. Fuller
University of North Carolina at Greensboro

The survey consists of 100 items representing the five P's of the Invitational Model, Persons (30 items), Places (20), Policies (20), Programs (10) and Processes (20). Some of the items are stated positively and others are stated negatively. The scoring depends on which way the item is stated, either one to five or five to one.

The different characteristics are factored out as follows:

People: 3, 8, 9, 11, 13, 16, 21, 23, 26, 28, 30, 33, 37, 40, 41, 50, 52, 58, 60, 63, 68, 69, 76, 79, 80, 82, 83, 84, 91, and 97.

Places: 4, 12, 14, 24, 25, 27, 31, 32, 38, 39, 43, 44, 53, 55, 62, 71, 73, 88, 89, and 92.

Policies: 1, 2, 6, 10, 17, 18, 19, 22, 42, 48, 57, 62, 65, 67, 72, 75, 85, 90, 98, and 100.

Programs: 5, 34, 36, 43, 45, 47, 74, 81, 95, and 96.

Processes: 7, 15, 20, 29, 35, 49, 51, 54, 56, 59, 64, 66, 70, 77, 78, 86, 87, 93, 94, and 99.

The Inviting School Survey

Please indicate your response to each of the following statements by placing a check in the one column that best represents your opinion of your school.

	Strongly Agree	Agree	Undecided	Disagree	Strongly Disagree
1. Rules in this school are fairly administered.					
2. Teachers are unwilling to help students who have special problems.					
3. People in this school have ample time to go to the bathroom.					
4. Furniture is unpleasant and uncomfortable.					
5. Everyone is encouraged to participate in athletic programs.					
6. School policy provides for assistance for those students who need it.					
7. Students work cooperatively with one another.					
8. Teachers express appreciation for students' presence in their classes.					
9. Custodians take pride in keeping the school as clean as possible.					
10. Special efforts are made to recognize the cultural contributions of minority groups.					
11. The principal involves everyone in the decision-making process.					
12. Soap and towels are available in student restrooms.					

	Strongly Agree	Agree	Undecided	Disagree	Strongly Disagree
13. Everyone in this school takes responsibility for keeping it clean.					
14. The air smells fresh in this school.					
15. Bathroom time is strictly scheduled into the school day.					
16. Teachers in this school show a lack of respect for students.					
17. Few, if any, students fail in this school.					
18. Tardiness is a problem in this school.					
19. Students have the opportunity to talk to one another during class activities.					
20. Students are pleased when they are called upon.					
21. Teachers are difficult to talk with.					
22. School policy permits and encourages freedom of expression of students, faculty, parents and administrators.					
23. People in this school laugh a lot.					
24. Observations indicate that space is cluttered and otherwise misused.					
25. The school grounds are clean and well-maintained.					
26. People in this school find ways to serve the surrounding community.					
27. There are many living green plants inside this school.					

	Strongly Agree	Agree	Undecided	Disagree	Strongly Disagree
28. Teachers take little or no time to talk with students about their out-of-class activities.					
29. Teachers and principals work cooperatively in this school.					
30. Teachers are generally prepared for class.					
31. The restrooms in this school are clean and properly maintained.					
32. Students like to visit the school library.					
33. Teachers exhibit a sense of humor.					
34. The lunch program at this school is a pleasant addition to the school day.					
35. Grades are assigned by means of fair and comprehensive assessment of work and effort.					
36. There is a school wellness program in this school.					
37. People in this school are impolite to one another.					
38. The library is open before and after school.					
39. The principal's or headmaster's office is attractive.					
40. Teachers work to encourage students' self-confidence.					
41. Teachers expect high academic performance from students.					
42. Signs posted in and around this school are positively worded.					

	Strongly Agree	Agree	Undecided	Disagree	Strongly Disagree
43. School programs involve out of school experience.					
44. Bulletin boards are attractive and up-to-date.					
45. The cafeteria food is unappetizing.					
46. Trash is left on school buses.					
47. Provisions are made for students of varying needs.					
48. Everyone in this school has a say in deciding school rules.					
49. All telephone calls to this school are answered promptly and politely.					
50. The principal treats people as though they are responsible.					
51. Everyone arrives on time for school.					
52. Creative thinking is encouraged in this school.					
53. Space is available for student independent study.					
54. Student discipline is approached from a positive standpoint.					
55. Fire alarm instructions are well-posted and seem reasonable.					
56. Music is played in gym classes during indoor exercise periods.					
57. The messages and notes sent home are positive.					
58. Teachers show insensitivity to the feelings of students.					

	Strongly Agree	Agree	Undecided	Disagree	Strongly Disagree
59. Teachers discuss planning and student process in teams.					
60. Students work cooperatively with each other.					
61. Teachers maintain clear and reasonable work standards.					
62. Classrooms offer a variety of furniture arrangements.					
63. People in this school want to be here.					
64. People often feel unwelcome when they enter the school facility.					
65. Communicating directly with this school is a difficult and time-consuming task.					
66. Much of this school's correspondence is negative in tone.					
67. Corporal punishment is used to punish students.					
68. Parents feel they are not welcome in this school.					
69. People in this school try to stop vandalism when they see it happening.					
70. Salad bar/salad/fresh fruit choices are available in the cafeteria.					
71. Clocks and water fountains are in good repair.					
72. The school intercom (P.A. System) interrupts classroom learning.					

	Strongly Agree	Agree	Undecided	Disagree	Strongly Disagree
73. The cafeteria is an unpleasant place to eat lunch.					
74. Good health practices are encouraged in this school.					
75. Few, if any, students fail in this school.					
76. Teachers appear to enjoy life.					
77. The school administrators show a strong interest in making this school inviting.					
78. Teachers use a variety of methods to help students learn.					
79. Teachers demonstrate a lack of enthusiasm about their work.					
80. The principal of this school knows the names of many students.					
81. Interruptions to classroom/ academic activities are kept to a minimum in this school.					
82. People in this school succeed in doing what is expected of them.					
83. School pride is evident among students.					
84. Teachers share out-of-class experiences with students.					
85. This school's policy provides for guidance in academic matters and athletic activities only.					
86. Only a select few in this school are involved in making decisions.					

	Strongly Agree	Agree	Undecided	Disagree	Strongly Disagree
87. Daily attendance by students, staff and faculty is high.					
88. Grass, evergreens, shrubs around the school are well-kept.					
89. There are comfortable chairs for visitors.					
90. Nutritious and health-promoting refreshments are served at school meetings.					
91. Teachers spend time after school with those who need extra help.					
92. The lighting in this school is more than adequate.					
93. People are ignored when they enter offices in this school.					
94. Classes get started quickly.					
95. The school sponsors extracurricular activities beyond sports.					
96. Mini courses are available to students.					
97. People in this school feel free to disagree with one another.					
98. School buses sometimes leave without waiting for students.					
99. People are discouraged from beginning new projects in this school.					
100. The grading practices in this school are unfair.					

Thank you for completing this survey.

Appendix B

The Alliance Honor Roll of Inviting Schools

The International Alliance for Invitational Education
c/o School of Education
University of North Carolina at Greensboro, NC 27412

THE ALLIANCE HONOR ROLL OF INVITING SCHOOLS

Do you know of an inviting school (yours or another's) that should be listed in the Alliance for Invitational Education Honor Roll of Inviting Schools?

A special committee of the Alliance has been selected to identify and honor inviting schools. Recipients of this honor will be listed in the Alliance Honor Roll of Inviting Schools, receive a special letter of commendation and an honor decal from the Alliance, will be recognized in the *Alliance Newsletter*, and at all Alliance Workshops and Conferences.

Schools nominated for this award will receive a survey questionnaire based on the inviting school research of Timothy Gerber, Ph.D. and others in the Alliance. The survey is to be completed by a school committee and returned to the Alliance Honor Roll Committee for consideration. To be considered for the award it is necessary for the school to be nominated by an Alliance member and to be accredited by a nationally recognized agency.

To nominate a school for this special honor, Alliance members are asked to send nominations to Honor Roll Chairperson, International Alliance for Invitational Education, c/o School of Education, University of North Carolina at Greensboro, NC 27412. Your nomination should include the principal or headmaster's name, the name and address of the school, and a detailed letter from you explaining the reasons for the nomination. Self nominations are encouraged. Nominations for the Honor Roll are accepted continuously. Each Alliance member may nominate ONE SCHOOL PER YEAR.

Think what it would mean for students if every school deserved the honor of displaying the "This is an Inviting School" decal.

Very best wishes,

Betty L. Siegal	William Watson Purkey
President	Professor
Kennesaw College	UNC-Greensboro
Co-Director	Co-Director

Schools Which Have Received
the Inviting School Award

(1989) Carlisle School, Box 5388, Martinsville, VA 24115.
Principal: Dick Hensley.

(1989) East Bend Elementary School, Box 129, East Bend,
NC 27018. Principal: Michael Crouse.

(1989) Fall Creek Elementary School, Rt. 1, Box 416A,
East Bend, NC 27018. Principal: Mrs. Barriere.

(1989) George W. Miller Elementary School, 50 Blauvelt
Road, Nanuet, NY 10954. Principal: Dr. Arline Gold.

(1989) Gotsch Intermediate School, 8348 South Laclede
Station Rd., St. Louis, MO 63123. Principal: Pamela
Sylvara.

(1989) Graham Middle School, Graham, NC 27253.
Principal: Sam Fowler.

(1989) H.B. Dupont Middle School, Meeting House &
Benge Rd., Hockessin, DE 19707. Principal: Francis
Ryan.

(1989) Kalayaan Elementary School, Box 70-K, FPO, San
Francisco 96651. Principal: Frank S. Vahovich, Ph.D.

(1989) Kishwaukee Elementary School, 526 Catlin St.,
Rockford, Il. 61108. Principal: Nancy R. Porter.

(1989) Meadowood School, 55-A S. Meadowood Dr.,
Newark, DE 19711. Principal: Floyd McDowell.

(1989) Oconee Co. Primary School, Box 468 Hog
Mountain Rd., Watkinsville, GA 30677. Principal: Dr.
Austine Wallis.

(1989) Shreve Elementary School, 598 N. Market St.,
Shreve, OH 44676. Principal: Robert D. Blanchard,
Ph.D.

(1989) Valley Elementary, 310 Opportunity Drive, Pelham,
AL 35124. Principal: Dr. Norma Rogers.

(1989) Vincent Massey Secondary School, 1800 Liberty
St., Windsor, Ontario, Canada, N9E 1J2. Principal: Val
Motuuk.

(1989) West Jefferson Elementary School, 26501 Barkley
Rd., Conifer, CO 80433. Principal: Cindy Smrz.

(1989) Wilmore-Davis Elementary, 7975 W. 41st, Wheat
Ridge, CO 80033. Principal: Dr. George Lauterbach.

(1989) Winston Churchill Collegiate Institute, 2239
Lawrence Ave. East, Scarborough, Ontario M1P 2P7.
Principal: J.D. Peacock.

(1988) American International School, Calle Oratorio,
4,07015, Mallorca, Spain. Headmaster: M. F. Pajares.

(1988) Anna P. Mote School, Edwards Ave. & Kirkwood HIWAY, Wilmington, DE 19808. Principal: Dale Schurr.

(1988) Boonville Elementary School, PO Box 129, Boonville, NC 27011. Principal: Frank Brown.

(1988) Hendrik Louw Primary School, PO Box 94, Strand 7140, South Africa. Principal: Gert J.J. Swart.

(1988) Jackson Alternative School, 766 Park Road, Jackson, MI 49204. Principal: Donald Tassie.

(1988) Kent County High School, RTS 297 & 298, Worton, MD 21678. Principal: David Kergaard.

(1988) Marbrook Elementary School, 2101 Centerville Rd., Wilmington, DE 19808. Principal: Linda Poole.

(1988) Murdock Elementary School, 2320 Murdock Rd., Marietta, GA 27412. Principal: Pete Robertson.

(1988) Parkview Elementary School, 773 Parkview Dr., Wooster, OH 44691. Principal: Lewis Stern.

(1988) Roaring Brook Elementary, Quaker Rd., Chappaqua, NY 10514. Principal: Mark Soss.

(1988) Satchel Ford Elementary School, 5901 Satchel Ford Rd., Columbia, SC 29202. Principal: Bernadette Scott.

(1988) Sedalia Elementary School, PO Box A, Sedalia, NC 27342. Principal: Peggy Johnson.

(1988) Shortlidge Elementary School, 18th & West St., Wilmington, DE 19802. Principal: Paul Julian.

(1988) Wendell Elementary GT Magnet School, PO Box 727, Wilson Ave., Wendell, NC 27591. Principal: Betsy Roundtree.

(1988) William E. Ferron School, 4200 Mountain Vistas, Las Vegas, NV 89121. Principal: Dr. Peggy Cahoon.

(1987) Bladen Elementary School, PO Box 638, 1300 Ben St., Elizabethtown, NC 28337. Principal: Donald Smith.

(1987) Brentfield Elementary School, 6767 Brentfield, Dallas, TX 75248. Principal: Harold Havard.

(1987) Broward Estates Elementary, 441 Northwest 35th Avenue, Fort Lauderdale, FL 33311. Principal: Bruce Voelkel.

(1987) Campus Learning Center, Potsdam College, SUNY, Potsdam, NY 13676. Director: Genevieve A. Baxter.

(1987) Cline Elementary School, 99 Virginia Ave., Centerville, OH 45459. Principal: Pat Buckingham.

(1987) (1986) Gateway Elementary School, Rt. 5, Hawkins Rd., Traveler's Rest, SC 29690. Principal: Glenn Wright.

(1987) Grand Heights Early Childhood Center, 2302 West Grand, Artesia, NM 88210. Principal: Kate Asbill.

(1987) North Elementary School, 500 Woodstock St.,
Crystal Lake, Il 60014. Principal: Hal Wajrowski.

(1987) Norwood Elementary, 1700 Delvale Ave., Dundalk,
MD 21222. Principal: Richard E. Fox.

(1987) Riverside Secondary School, 8465 Jerome St.,
Windsor, Ontario, Canada N8S 1W8. Principal: R.D.
Creech.

(1987) Rosedale, 25 Erindale Ave., Hamilton, Canada L8K
4R1. Principal: Larry Evans.

(1987) Saint Charles Borromeo, 4600 Ackerman Blvd.,
Kettering, OH 45429. Principal: Karen Sammons, S.C.

(1987) Sugar Loaf, Rte. 1, Box 225, Taylorsville, NC
28681. Principal: Joel Blackburn.

(1987) Taylor High School, 30-36 Harrison Ave., North
Bend, OH 45052. Principal: Jimmie Dunbar.

(1987) Thoroughgood Elementary School, 1444 Dunstan
Lane, Virginia Beach, VA 23345. Principal: Ralph
Mizelle.

(1987) Walter J. Kossman School, 90 Flocktown Rd., Long
Valley, NJ 07055. Principal: Nancy Evans.

(1987) West Yadkin Elementary, Rt. 3, Box A,
Hamptonville, NC 27020. Principal: Jack Williams.

(1987) Yadkinville Elementary School, PO Box 518,
Yadkinville, NC 27055. Principal: Roger Nixon.

(1986) Chester Goodridge Elementary, PO Box #37 Conner
Road, Hebron, KY 41048. Principal: Paul Champion.

(1986) Guilford Elementary School, 411 Friendway Road,
Greensboro, NC 27410. Principal: Doris Henderson.

(1986) Millis Road Elementary School, 4310 Millis Road,
Jamestown, NC 27282. Principal: Wanda H. Szensay.

(1986) Orange County High, Selma Rd., Orange, VA
22960. Principal: Paul Cogar.

(1986) Primrose School, Rt. 139, Lincolndale, NY 10540.
Principal: James Beaty.